Advice to a Young Critic
AND OTHER LETTERS

Bernard Shaw, about 1900

Advice to a Young Critic

AND OTHER LETTERS

BY BERNARD SHAW

Notes and Introduction by E. J. West

CROWN PUBLISHERS, INC.
NEW YORK

Manufactured in the United States of America
by American Book–Stratford Press, Inc., N. Y.

Contents

v

Throughout these letters the editor has kept Shaw's original spellings, which are sometimes, especially in proper names, incorrect. However, a few obvious typographical errors in the original have been silently corrected.

Because of the stipulation in Bernard Shaw's will that "heed must be taken both to the credit and feeling of any living person," it was necessary to abridge slightly Letters 38, 40 and 69.

Introduction

This new collection of Bernard Shaw letters is not, frankly, all of a piece. Starting definitely as what may well be called "advice to a young critic," the letters changed as the years passed and the interests of both Shaw and Reginald Golding Bright, and the relationship between the two, changed greatly, but the early letters are among the most illuminating concerning Shaw and the history of his early plays that have yet been published. (One pauses parenthetically to lament that there must be literally thousands of letters written by Shaw that have not yet been made public, and the good Shavian shudders at the thought of the hundreds probably of great interest that may have been destroyed or never will be made public.)

What is a good Shavian? Since the main interest of the present volume will be for him, it seems worthwhile attempting to define him. I can only paraphrase some words I wrote about five years ago in the course of a review of a book of Shavian biography and criticism. Shortly before his death on November 1, 1950, Shaw, in a preface to fellow-Fabian G. D. H. Cole's volume of selections from Samuel Butler, stated that Darwin was no more a Darwinist than he himself was a Shavian. Like most of his pronouncements, this was multiple-barreled. But among other things Shaw surely meant that in his mid-nineties he was not an academic researcher amid the vast and still constantly increasing library of comment and criticism, of debate and diatribe, of biography and bunk, written about himself. In that sense Shaw was not a Shavian. Refusing a year before his death to read a review of his neighbor Winsten's confused and confusing book about him and of his own *Sixteen Self Sketches* sent to him by one of my editors, G. B. S. explained: "The Shavian Essayists are often not only good friends and faithful fans, but interesting authors on their own account. But they should be read for their own sakes, not for mine." In the sense that I am myself a Shavian, I would define the term as meaning one who is still a good friend to Shaw (although not necessarily one actually acquainted during his lifetime) a faithful fan, and an avid reader of the works of the Shavian Essayists. And one must insist that not all of the latter have been good Shavians (with critical integrity necessary to him who has closely studied the critical tenets and the critical credo of the Master himself, one must deny the title, for instance, to G. K. Chesterton, Archibald Henderson, Frank Harris, Stephen Winsten, and Louis Kronenberger). Wherefore this new volume of intimate personal revelation becomes the more valuable. And if it would seem that I am defending myself, I assert that while it is not the necessary business of an editor to be an "interesting author," nothing is lost in this instance by his being a good Shavian.

The present volume lacks the combined graces of style, of personal emotional appeal and of give-and-take of the correspondence with the inimitable Ellen Terry and the unpredictable Mrs. Pat Campbell, but the early letters as a group and many of the later ones are written in Shaw's best vein, if not in his most perfect style; they provide much additional evidence of some of his finer qualities and characteristics; and they either offer really new information or firmly settle hitherto moot points concerning his career and his works.

The first and the third letters, for instance, sound out conclusively Shaw's steady critical credo, already by 1894 well thought out during years of reviewing of musical performances, and to be religiously followed and developed during his years as dramatic critic: integrity and fair-mindedness combined, security of the critical self, respect for the performer or performing organization criticized. The third, dated December 2, 1894, with the accompanying manuscript of Bright, is probably unique as an example of meticulously careful and purely gratuitous and altruistic editing of the work of a beginner by a truly established critic of the arts, if as yet an untried full-fledged dramatic critic. It is one of the most important examples of pure statement and of pure style that I have encountered, even in Shaw's own words.

The fourth entry, dated December 14, 1894, is, like so many letters in this new collection, equally notable for pointed practical advice and for illuminating self-revelation. As Shaw tirelessly repeated during his active writing life (the first letter was written during his thirty-eighth year and he died in his ninety-fifth), he was always generous with autobiographical details, but even to the tireless Shavian researcher this volume presents new, necessary, and indispensable Shavian material.

For example, if the ever-generous and reliably charitable Shaw had any real *bêtes noires* during his long critical career, surely they were the fictional Paula Tanqueray of Sir Arthur Wing Pinero and the indubitably real and English Brodribb who was to become, shortly after this correspondence began, and partly, one more than suspects, at the instance of a well-known critic famous as G. B. S., Sir Henry Irving. The letter of April 22, 1895, attempting to argue young Bright out of his worship of his "Dulcinea," Paula Tanqueray, and the self-interview, dated May 15, 1897, concerning the much-debated matter of Irving's refusal to produce Shaw's *The Man of Destiny*, therefore, would by themselves make this volume invaluable to all future students of late nineteenth-century dramatic and theatrical history and criticism.

II.

If the true Shavian be, as I have posited, an indefatigable reader of all that concerned Shaw in any way, it will be obvious that I reacted with enormous interest and equal impatience some two years ago to announcement of two publications, one English, the correspondence of Bernard Shaw with R. Golding Bright, "The Inner History of His Plays," and one American, Bernard Shaw, *Advice to a Young Critic*. It was, therefore, with something more than approaching real alarm that I discovered myself three months ago embarked upon the editing of both volumes, which turned out to be identical. Let me express my gratitude to the following for help in finishing the task: the great critic, John Gassner; Eric J. Batson, secretary of The Shaw Society of London, who labored under pressure in London to do the work there that I should myself have undertaken; George Freedley, Curator of the Theatre Collection of the New York Public Library; and various of my colleagues here in the foothills of the Rockies who uncomplainingly answered—usually over the telephone—numerous and usually unexplained strange questions. I suppose some credit also must be given to one of the most inexplicable inventions of the modern world, the researching mind, that accumulator of unconsidered, if not eventually inconsiderable, scraps of information, trifles so handy in annotating at top-speed and in the midst of the pressure of the graduate-degree mill such a volume as this.

To my scholarly disconcertion, my most difficult task was discovering something about the man to whom Shaw wrote these letters. For, as I have noted, and as I would re-emphasize, this volume presents a one-sided correspondence. One manuscript (printed? who knows? not I) and several printed notices of R. E. Golding Bright are included, as are several business notes from Shaw to Elisabeth Marbury, American play-agent whose London office Bright managed after the death of his elder brother, and to Ada Wooldridge, secretary in that office. (The correspondence was selected and put together from the files of Golding Bright, by Miss Joan Ling, herself now a London play-agent.) Apparently either Bright did not bother to save, or his executrix to copy, his own side of the correspondence, and it is distinctly obvious that with Shaw's overwhelming correspondence, *he* could not afford to keep Bright's letters.

As a note to the first entry suggests, not even that amazingly assiduous biographer Hesketh Pearson seems to have been aware of this correspondence, and Eric Batson has written me that many informed Londoners "did not realize that G. B. *had* been Shaw's agent for so long!" Aside from one reference to him by Pearson, noted in my first separate commentary, Bright has never been mentioned by name in a work on Shaw, although, as I point out later, Shaw himself did, in a letter to Ellen Terry dated May 13, 1897, anonymously mention "a young journalist in whom I am interested" to whom he had given the dialogue of the interview with Irving concerning *The Man of Destiny.* Until the publication of the present volume, that reference has meant nothing to Shavian students.

Most of the data in the younger man's career relevant to the matters mentioned in the letters it has seemed best to use as commentary for the letters to which they apply, but the general reader might prefer some superficial briefing here. The father of Golding Bright was a doctor, as had been many of his ancestors (one, Dr. Richard Bright, having in 1827 identified and named Bright's disease), residing at 153 Sunderland Road, Forest Hill, London, S.E. Golding, born some time in 1874 before April 14th, was working in an office in The City when he first wrote to Shaw. The reader of these letters will note Shaw's sympathy with young Bright's desire to get out of the office, he himself having been a clerk, and a very successful one, in a Dublin estate agent's office in the early seventies. Bright's father obviously did not approve of his ambition to become a dramatic critic, possibly because an older brother, Arthur Addison, had already become both a journalist and, at least as early as 1891, an actor's agent and play broker. The course of Golding Bright's career up to the beginning of 1928 is made clear in the following letters or in the annotations. When Elisabeth Marbury died in 1933, he went on with his work as London representative of The American Play Company and was working in the same capacity for the Richard J. Madden Play Company at the time of his death.

My London correspondent reported that Bright was "pub-
licity-shy" (I later hazard the conjecture that this may have
been the result not only of temperament but also of reaction
to Addison's suicide on May 29, 1906), and neither my London
correspondent nor Lennox Robinson, the proposed editor of the
English edition of this correspondence, was able to find out
much about Bright in London. It is evident, however, that in
his later years he was a well-known figure at London first-
nights, one of distinction and dignity, with silvery short hair
and a charming smile, always sitting in the same stall, always
in immaculate evening dress, with the swinging black cape, top
hat, white gloves, and gold-headed cane of a bygone era. Eric
Batson informs me that, according to London gossip, at these
first-nights he "often went to sleep!" So, for that matter, did
Shaw's great friend, that respected critic, William Archer, so
often to be referred to in this volume. But Mr. Batson goes on
to record of Bright that, unlike Archer: "When he awoke he
would forecast pretty exactly how long the play would run."
Viola Meynell, in her edition of *Letters of J. M. Barrie* (1947),
included four and a half pages of letters from Barrie to Bright,
dealing mainly with matters of the filming of the Scot's plays.
Arnold Bennett referred to Bright in passing three times in his
Journals, twice as agent, once as husband of "George Egerton."
Lady Cynthia Asquith, in her recent *Portrait of Barrie,* recorded
that all matters concerning production of the plays, while she
was Barrie's secretary, were referred to his "trusted agent,"
Golding Bright. Barrie, as we shall see later, had remained to
the very end the loyal friend of the older brother, Addison.
Elisabeth Marbury, in her reminiscences, *My Crystal Ball*
(1923), noted her sense of "extreme good fortune" in persuading Golding to assume Addison's position, on the latter's death,
as her London representative and spoke of him admiringly if
briefly: "He keeps ahead of his time. He was born a modern.
His judgment as to the merit of a manuscript is rarely at fault."

The little that I have been able to find out about Golding
Bright, recorded in the notes or summarized above, accords

with an appreciation of him by the late Valentine Williams, published in The London *Times* ten days after his death. It suggests in maturity a personality but faintly shadowed forth by the brash young man who forced himself upon the attention of Shaw on the night of April 21, 1894, and who wrote to him soon thereafter for the first time. One laments in reading this tribute from a friend, as frequently when reading Shaw's letters to him, that "My dear G. B."'s side of the correspondence is not also available. For one gathers there was in the brash youth of twenty something which suggested to the intuitive Shaw the charm of personality of the man who died at sixty-seven, and of whom Williams in The London *Times* of April 24, 1941, wrote:

> With the death on Easter Monday after a long illness of Golding Bright the theatre in England and America has lost one of its best-known and most influential figures. For many years London's leading play agent, his notable list of clients included J. M. Barrie, Bernard Shaw, and Somerset Maugham. But Golding Bright was a great deal more than a shrewd and capable dramatic agent with an unrivalled knowledge of the theatre in all its aspects, who looked after his clients' interests with unremitting zeal. His judgment of a play was rarely at fault, and his great experience was frequently called upon by playwrights and managers alike in the difficult period that lies between the writing of a play and its presentation in the theatre. Many well-known actors and actresses owe their careers to his flair for casting. He was a familiar figure at London first nights, and "Golding" in his stall will be greatly missed. The deep sympathy of his host of friends will go out to his wife, the distinguished writer "George Egerton," his devoted companion during 40 years of married life, who nursed him at his express wish during his last illness.

Were the mere editor of a volume of letters permitted a dedication, mine would be to the author of these letters, and for the inscription I would repeat some words I wrote to Eric

Batson a couple of years ago: "Alive he haunted me. Dead he
seems more alive than ever." After living intensively and intensely with these letters for a bare three months, I would
repeat these words with greater and more passionate sincerity.
I have loved the man for some forty years, just this side of
idolatry. The editing of this volume—however inadequately
carried out, and I think I realize its shortcomings better than
any other man will—has been a labor of love in the ultimate
sense. I beg from Shaw's reverend shade and from his still
living and breathing personality pardon for any sins of commission or omission. What sins there be, venial or mortal, they
are mine alone. *Mea apologia?* No. *Mea culpa.*

E. J. WEST

Boulder, Colorado
September 5, 1955

I. ON CRITICISM AND
DRAMATIC COMMENTARY

1. On Becoming a Critic and on *Arms and the Man*

Private

29 Fitzroy Square, W.
30th April, 1894.

Dear Sir

Your letter has only just reached me. They did not forward it from the theatre, expecting a visit from me every day.

There is no way of becoming a dramatic critic. It happens by accident. For instance, I have never been offered a post of the kind, though I should have been quite willing to take it any time these last eighteen years. But when the accident happens, it happens to a journalist. It is to men who are already in the profession, and known as men who can write and who know the ways of papers, that editors turn when a vacancy occurs. If you work for a paper as a reporter or paragraphist, and are keen on theatres, you can generally do a stray notice on an emergency which makes you known to the editor as having a turn that way. Then, if the dramatic critic dies, or goes on another paper, or drops journalism, you have your chance of succeeding him, if you have shown the requisite capacity. That is the regular way. But you may induce some friend who starts a paper, or becomes editor of one, to give you a trial straight off; but that is a matter of pure luck, with, of course, the skill to take the luck when it comes. Remember, to be a critic, you must be not only a bit of an expert in your subject, but you must also have literary skill, and trained critical skill

3

too—the power of analysis, comparison &c. I have had to go through years of work as a reviewer of books, a critic of pictures, a writer on political & social questions, and a musical critic, in order to qualify myself for the post I now hold on the staff of The World. You must not think that because you only heard of me for the first time the other day or thereabouts that I got such reputation as I have cheaply. I came to London in 1876, and have been fighting for existence ever since. Even my little platform performance at the Playgoers' Club was the result of about fifteen years practice of public speaking, mostly under the humblest circumstances. I tell you this lest you should be discouraged and embittered by thinking that you are meeting with exceptional and unfair difficulties. In London all beginners are forty, with twenty years of obscure hard work behind them; and, believe me, those obscure twenty years are not the worst part of one's life, nor need you nor anyone be afraid to face them.

I still hold to it that a man who thinks a dramatic performance worth waiting at the pit door all day for is a lunatic. The front row of the pit is worth something; but it is not worth that. However, I only give you my own valuation. If your enthusiasm makes it worth the trouble to you, I have no right to object.

All the views which you attribute to me concerning Mr. Irving and Mr. Tree and the "new school" have, if you will excuse me saying so, been put into your mind by newspaper paragraphs written by people who have not the slightest knowledge of me or my views. There is nothing that annoys me more than all this nonsense about new schools & the new drama & the rest of it. I suffer from it considerably, as it leads people to construe purely dramatic passages in my plays as interpolations of what are supposed to be my political views. But even if the play did contain any such interpolation, I should not admit your right to make a disturbance on the head of it. If the Fabians in the gallery were enjoying my play, as I am glad to say that the gallery still does now that there are no longer any Fabians in it, why did you carry your disapproval of a purely imaginary allusion to the Royal Family to the point of making them lose patience with you? Have they ever disturbed you in the enjoyment of the patriotic and loyal sentiments with which popular melodramas are freely spiced? We have both been present, I have no doubt, at first nights of plays containing a good deal that is exceedingly repugnant to my political & moral opinions. I don't think you have ever found me interrupting an actor or annoying my neighbours on that account. I simply do not go to the sort of plays I dislike.

In conclusion, let me assure you that I did my best to put before you a true picture of what a brave soldier who knows his business really is. I heartily wish you could bring me an audience of veterans—of men who know what it is to ride a bolting horse in a charge, or to trust to the commissariat for food during a battle, or to be under fire for two or three days: they would not have taken my chocolate &c &c for silly jokes, as I feel a good many of the audience did.

Yours faithfully

G. Bernard Shaw

Shaw's *Arms and the Man,* a romantic comedy in three acts, was presented by the actress Florence Farr, who played Louka, at the Avenue Theatre, London, April 21, 1894. On the opening night Bernard Gould, who was playing Sergius, is reported to have substituted "British" for "Bulgarian" in an uncomplimentary remark about the Bulgarian army, and a youth in the gallery hissed. Later, when Shaw appeared at the end of the play for a curtain call, the same youth gave a loud and solitary "Boo!" Shaw, long since accustomed as a public speaker to heckling, immediately replied with one of his most famous pieces of impromptu repartee: "My dear fellow, I quite agree with you; but what are we two against so many?" Hesketh Pearson claimed in 1942, without citing his evidence, that the "unknown lad" who hissed and booed was actually Golding Bright, whom he identified only by name and whom he never mentioned again in his biography of Shaw. One assumes that Shaw had at some time given Pearson the identification, but had not mentioned the long correspondence with Bright. The apparently ambiguous comments in the penultimate paragraph of this first letter about Bright's making a "disturbance" in the gallery and the date of the letter, however, now make quite certain, first, that the long-told story of the fractious galleryite is not apocryphal, and second, that the youth was indeed Golding Bright. The reference to Shaw's "little platform performance at the Playgoers' Club" might seem to suggest that the two men had met there, but the letter of November 11, 1895 (Number 9) shows that at least up to that time Shaw did not know Bright even by sight. With both parties dead, how can we settle this problem? It seems to me quite possible that a youth of sufficient freshness (of whatever kind) to buck the Fabians in the gallery with the hiss and the majority of the audience with the booing (his eventual and long-time boss Elisabeth Marbury in her reminiscences reported of Bright as late as 1923 that he would "always be a young man at any age") may well have taken the opportunity of having forced himself anonymously upon Shaw's attention as an excuse to identify himself in the letter to which this first one by Shaw is an obvious response.

And now I must make a confession: legends accumulate about such a figure as Shaw even in his lifetime, and I obviously as editor of this intriguing but all too frequently enigmatic one-sided correspondence run the risk of perpetrating more legends upon him dead. I give Bernard Gould's slip of the tongue on the authority of Hesketh Pearson, a rather cavalier guide in any matter, and one who in this matter could speak most certainly only from hearsay, not from observation. I happen to know *Arms and the Man* very intimately, but I have rechecked and will guarantee that Sergius never mentions the Bulgarian army. On the other hand, I can find no passage which young Bright could, in Shaw's words, have interpreted as an "allusion to the Royal Family." Surely it could not have been, "Swiss civilization nursetending British [slip-of-the-tongue for the intended Bulgarian] barbarism, eh?" No, that's too far-fetched. Yet it is the only line spoken by Sergius that seems in any way to satisfy Shaw's immediate and Pearson's legendary explanation of the reason for the hiss.

To matters of fact: The Playgoers' Club, ten years old in 1894, of which obviously Golding Bright was an active member, was a group of young people interested in the theatre, who attended many plays, frequently as a group, and who held meetings at which they seriously discussed the theatre and the drama or listened to addresses by critics or players. . . . Mr. Irving was, of course, the greatest English actor of the later nineteenth century, the great lord of the Lyceum, the original Henry Brodribb who was very soon to become Sir Henry Irving, and who seems to have been during Shaw's long lifetime his only real *bête noire*. Mr. Tree was Herbert Beerbohm Tree, at the time only recently become a member of the actor-manager group, who was himself to become the even more eccentric lord of Her Majesty's (later His Majesty's), and himself to be knighted. . . . The "new school," written in quotes in 1894, did not refer to the new drama which Shaw mentions, but to the then incumbent descendants of the "modern," "realistic" school of acting which the playwright Tom Robertson and the acting team of Marie and Squire Bancroft had established in the 1860's in deliberate opposition to the old traditional, classical methods of training which had produced successively such figures as Thomas Betterton, David Garrick, the Kemble family and their bright particular star Mrs. Sarah Siddons, Edmund Kean, W. C. Macready, and Samuel Phelps. Probably the finest examples of the new school in the 1890's were John Hare and Madge Kendal and her husband.

This first letter in this first-published collection is one of the best and is typically Shavian in many respects: the generosity evident in the promptness of the reply (the date is little over a week beyond the opening night of the play), the lack of acrimony toward an unknown young man who had made a "disturbance," the seriousness with which the unknown's problems are considered, the very length of the letter, and especially the personal quality throughout—the fine critical credo, the frank summary of his own career, and the gentleness of such reproof as is offered. Shaw was at the time of writing still continuing, under the initials G. B. S., as music critic for *The World*, the career he had begun on *The*

Star in 1888, under T. P. O'Connor, with the pseudonym of "Corno di Bassetto." . . . The defense of the realism of *Arms and the Man* in the concluding paragraph suggests the remark that surely Shaw must already have written or was contemplating writing an important and almost forgotten long essay on the same subject which was to appear in *The New Review* for July, "A Dramatic Realist to His Critics," in which almost every point in the play, from Bluntschli's passion for chocolate creams to his strange proposal to Raina at the end, was shown to be founded on actual reality.

2. Some Personal Data and Encouragement to the Fledgling Journalist

LETTER CARD

Post Mark:
Nov. 19/'94.

To: R. E. Golding Bright Esq.
The Playgoers' Club,
409 Strand,
W.C.

29 Fitzroy Square, W.
19th November, 1894.

Dear Sir

Your letter surprised me, because, as it happened, I had just sent your name to an editor who wanted a dramatic critic; and it seemed odd that we should think of one another simultaneously. However, as the position in question—that of the criticship of The Saturday Review under Frank Harris—was one which could only as a very bold experiment have been given to a comparatively untried hand, Harris was probably more disposed to damn my eyes for refusing the berth myself than to entertain my suggestion of an alternative.

By all means make the Sun pay you. But if you can afford it, let the account run until it is large enough to save the appearance of worrying about a trifle—say until it is over a couple of pounds or so. Never allow a regular commercial newspaper to get copy from you for nothing; but never, either, if you can avoid it, show any anxiety about being paid. Take it as a matter of course that what is worth publishing is worth paying for.

The title "Mrs. Jarman's Profession" is a curious illustration of the influence of Paula Tanqueray. The real title is "Mrs. Warren's Profession." The name Jarman never came into my head, nor is there any authority for it except some association of ideas in Grein's head which led him to give the wrong name to his interviewer.

My separation from The World is permanent. I made up my mind to take the opportunity of Edmund Yates's death to escape from musical criticism, which is not so amusing to the writer who has written a long article on the subject for seven years as it is to his readers. I have an article on musical criticism in a forthcoming number of The Scottish Musical Monthly. I will ask the editor to send you a copy.

My successor Mr. Hitchens (or whatever his name is) seems to me to write cleverly & pleasantly enough. You must give up detesting everything appertaining to Oscar Wilde or to anyone else. The critic's first duty is to admit, with absolute respect, the right of every man to his own style. Wilde's wit and his fine literary workmanship are points of great value. There is always a vulgar cry both for and against every man or woman of any distinction; and from such cries you cannot keep your mind too clear if you wish to attain distinction yourself. You know the sort of thing I mean: you have heard it about Whistler, Sarah Grand, Ibsen, Wagner—everybody who has a touch of genius. Excuse this scrap of sermon: I would not intrude it upon you if I did not know by experience the great difficulty of forming and holding to a genuine original opinion of public men on their own merits when so many fools are chattering about them in all directions.

Keep up your courage: from what you tell me you are getting on very well as far as the papers are concerned. But you ought to write a couple of books on the drama. Burn them afterwards by all means; but write them. I started by writing five books, one after the other, without producing the least impression on an apparently implacable destiny.

I am overwhelmed with work in connection with the School-board & Vestry elections & have only time to send this hastiest of scrawls.

Yours faithfully,
G. Bernard Shaw.

This letter is exceedingly interesting throughout. Edmund Yates, famous journalist and editor of *The World,* had died on May 19, and Shaw had reluctantly continued at his post as music critic until the end of the season in the autumn. The notorious Frank Harris had bought *The Saturday Review* in September and had immediately tried to hire the famous initials G. B. S. to appear at the foot of the dramatic column when he found that William Archer, Shaw's good friend who had first gotten him established as a critic of the arts, would not leave *The World.* It has been known that Shaw hesitated, but I do not believe it has been known as yet that with typical generosity he refused in order to suggest his epistolary disciple and public hisser and booer for the position. Harris obviously—and fortunately—ignored this gambit, pursued Shaw, and eventually persuaded him to begin in January, 1895, the series of criticisms which were to continue until May, 1898, and prove Shaw one of the great dramatic critics of all time.

Golding Bright had, some time in the little over six months since he first baited Shaw for advice, obviously found himself at least some work as a contributor of "gossip" paragraphs to *The Sun,* submitting them possibly as what we might call a voluntary free-lancer, as the second paragraph suggests. (A friend in London, Eric Batson, has been given to understand that Golding's older brother, Arthur Addison Bright, of whom we must learn much more later, had worked on *The Sun*, and was instrumental in helping Golding to take over the same job.) Now that his pupil is at least getting into print, Shaw typically gives practical advice.

At the time that Aubrey Tanqueray first met the professional courtesan who was to become his second wife, in Arthur Wing Pinero's famous play which so delightfully shook the dovecotes in the Parish of St. James's in 1893, she was living with a friend of his named Peter Jarman as his wife. Mrs. Warren, in Shaw's play, was, of course, no longer a prostitute but the owner of a great international chain of expensive and fashionable brothels. . . . J. T. Grein, a prosperous Dutch immigrant and devotee of the theatre, after active work as member and president of the Playgoers' Club, in 1891 founded the Independent Stage Society, an attempt to provide an English "free theatre" on the model of those in France and Germany. The first production, March 13, 1891, was the now historically famous *succès de scandale*, *Ghosts*, with that fine nonprofesional, Mrs. Theodore Wright, as Mrs. Alving. Grein was responsible for urging Shaw to finish the script of *Widowers' Houses*, which he had begun in 1885 in collaboration with William Archer. The play was produced by the Society at the Royalty Theatre, December 9 and 13, 1892. Shaw's actress friend, Florence Farr, to whom he wrote some famous letters and who later produced *Arms and the Man*, played Blanche Sartorius, and James Welch, who was to become a famous character comedian, made his first London appearance as Lickcheese.

I have never found the article on musical criticism, which many of us Shavians would value highly, nor can I find mention of it elsewhere than in this letter and the next. . . . Shaw was quite right to question his spelling of the name of his successor as music critic on *The World*; actually he was Robert Smythe Hichens, trained as a musician, but eventually to become a famous popular novelist, probably best known for *The Garden of Allah* and *Bella Donna*. . . . The passage on Wilde illustrates Shaw's generosity and his principles of disinterested criticism. The relationship between Shaw and Wilde, both personal and opinionative, was a long and complicated one, but, at least on Shaw's side, even during the time of the famous trial and afterward, it was always more than tolerant and understanding. Only once did he fail to appreciate Wilde—he was apparently the *only* critic who did not like *The Importance of Being Earnest.* (See his review under date of February 23, 1895, in *Our Theatres in the Nineties,* I.41-44.) . . . "Madame" Sarah Grand, as Shaw usually called her, was the author of a novel, *The Heavenly Twins,* which had made a great sensation with readers of the early nineties simply because its heroine, having married a former rake, deserted him on the wedding day when she learned the truth. This reversal of the normal Victorian male-female relationship caused the sensation. Where the normal reader professed to be shocked by the novel but read and re-read it, Shaw was delighted with the unorthodox point of view, with the defense of the New Woman, and he continually championed it and its author, using both again and again, especially in his dramatic criticism, as touchstones, as points of reference, as ethical and economic standards or yardsticks.

Shaw's "five books" were by no means "books on the drama." They were, of course, the famous five novels, written between 1879 and 1883, turned down by all standard publishers, four of them attaining serial publications in minor journals only after some years, and the earliest, *Immaturity,* appearing first only in the Standard Edition in 1930.

3. A Lesson in Practical Criticism: Shaw Edits a Bright Review

Private.   29 Fitzroy Square W.
                                           2nd December 1894.
Dear Sir

　　The best service I can do you is to take your notice and jot down on it without ceremony the comments which occur

to me. You will find first certain alterations in black ink. In
them I have tried to say, as well as I can off hand, what you
were trying to say: that is, since it was evident you were
dodging round some point or other, I have considered the only
point there was to make, and have made it. It came quite easy
when I had altered your statement about Frenchmen at large
to what you really meant—the conventional stage Frenchman.
Always find out rigidly and exactly what you mean, and never
strike an attitude, whether national or moral or critical or anything else. You struck a national attitude when you wrote that
about the Frenchman and Englishman; and you struck a moral
attitude when you wrote "She has sunk low enough in all conscience." Get your facts right first: that is the foundation of
all style, because style is the expression of yourself; and you
cannot express yourself genuinely except on a basis of precise
reality.

In red ink you will find some criticisms which you may
confidently take as expressing what an experienced editor
would think of your sample of work.

You have not at all taken in my recommendation to write a
book. You say you are scarcely competent to write books just
yet. That is just why I recommend you to learn. If I advised
you to learn to skate, you would not reply that your balance
was scarcely good enough yet. A man learns to skate by stag-
gering about and making a fool of himself. Indeed he pro-
gresses in all things by resolutely making a fool of himself.
You will never write a good book until you have written some
bad ones. If they have sent you my Scottish article, you will
see that I began by writing some abominably bad criticisms.
I wrote five long books before I started again on press work.
William Archer wrote a long magnum opus on the life and
works of Richard Wagner, a huge novel, and a book on the
drama, besides an essay on Irving and a good deal of leader
work for a Scotch paper before he began his victorious career
on The World. He also perpetrated about four plays in his
early days. (By the way, you mustn't publish this information).

You must go through that mill too; and you can't possibly start too soon. Write a thousand words a day for the next five years for at least nine months every year. Read all the great critics— Ruskin, Richard Wagner, Lessing, Lamb and Hazlitt. Get a ticket for the British Museum reading room, and live there as much as you can. Go to all the first rate orchestral concerts and to the opera, as well as to the theatres. Join debating societies and learn to speak in public. Haunt little Sunday evening political meetings and exercise that accomplishment. Study men and politics in this way. As long as you stay in the office, try and be the smartest hand in it: I spent four and a half years in an office before I was twenty. Be a teetotaller; don't gamble; don't lend; don't borrow; don't for your life get married; make the attainment of EFFICIENCY your sole object for the next fifteen years; and if the city can teach you nothing more, or demands more time than you can spare from your apprenticeship, tell your father that you prefer to cut loose and starve, and do it. But it will take you at least a year or two of tough work before you will be able to build up for yourself either the courage or the right to take heroic measures. Finally, since I have given you all this advice, I add this crowning precept, the most valuable of all. NEVER TAKE ANYBODY'S ADVICE.

And now, to abandon the role of your guide, philosopher and friend, which I don't propose to revert to again until you report progress in ten years or so, let me thank you for the paragraph in the Sun, which was quite right and appropriate. I have no more news at present, except that I have nearly finished a new play, the leading part in which I hope to see played by Miss Janet Achurch, of whose genius I have always had a very high opinion. It is quite a sentimental play, which I hope to find understood by women, if not by men; and it is so straightforward that I expect to find it pronounced a miracle of perversity. This is my fifth dramatic composition. The first was "Widowers' Houses" of Independent Theatre Fame. The second was "The Philanderer," a topical comedy in which the

New Woman figured before Mr. Grundy discovered her. The third was "Mrs. Warren's Profession," a play with a purpose, the purpose being much the same as that of my celebrated letter to the Pall Mall Gazette on the Empire controversy. The fourth was "Arms and the Man," which was so completely misunderstood that it made my reputation as a playwright both here and in New York. The Independent Theatre has already announced "Mrs. Warren's Profession" for its forthcoming season. "The Philanderer" was written originally for that society; but on its completion I threw it aside and wrote another more suitable for the purposes of the society—Mrs. Warren. Wyndham asked me to do something for him on seeing "Arms and the Man"; and I tried to persuade him to play The Philanderer; but whilst the project was under consideration, Wyndham made such a decisive success with "Rebellious Susan" that he resolved to follow up the vein of comedy opened by Henry Arthur Jones to the end before venturing upon the Shawian quicksand. But this involved so long a delay that I withdrew the play, and am now looking round to see whether the world contains another actor who can philander as well as Wyndham. As I have always said that if I did not write six plays before I was forty I would never write one after, I must finish the work now in hand and another as well before the 26th July 1896; but I hope to do much more than that, since I have managed to get through the present play within three months, during which I have had to take part in the Schoolboard and Vestry elections, to keep up my work in the Fabian Society, to deliver nearly two dozen lectures in London and the provinces, and to fire off various articles and criticisms. The fact is, I took a good holiday in Germany, Italy, and in Surrey; and I accumulated a stock of health which I am dissipating at a frightful rate. The Christmas holidays will come just in time to save my life.

If any of this stuff is of use to you for paragraphing purposes —and remember that the world will not stand too much Bernard Shaw—you are welcome to work it up by all means when it suits you. Only, don't quote it as having been said by me. That is an easy way out which I bar.

I find that you have got an atrociously long letter out of me. I have been blazing away on the platform this evening for an hour and a half, and ought to be in bed instead of clattering at this machine.

yours, half asleep,
G. Bernard Shaw

R. Golding Bright, Esq.
Playgoers' Club.

The above letter itself and the carefully edited Bright review which follows, form together, if it were needed, a very striking example of the painstaking care with which Shaw, a produced playwright, a music critic who had aroused general interest even among readers not interested in his subject from 1888 through 1894, a man himself about to take up the post of dramatic critic on *The Saturday Review,* and one of the best known public figures in London, tried to help by wise advice and practical aid a fledgling journalist.

Personally, I lament again the apparent loss of that "Scottish article." I trust some researching Shavian may eventually rescue it from the files, if these still survive, of *The Scottish Musical Monthly.* William Archer, Shaw's close friend for some forty years and fellow-critic during the late eighties and the nineties, according to his biographer-brother, Lieutenant-Colonel C. Archer, pursued his "elaborate study" of Wagner and his theories to an "advanced stage," but dropped the project when no publishers could be interested. The "huge novel" never appeared, and the brother does not mention it. The "book on the drama," I assume, was *English Dramatists of Today,* 1882, important historically as the first full volume in England devoted entirely to contemporary dramatists (granted, except for W. S. Gilbert, most of the men considered are now forgotten except by specialists). There were actually two essays on Irving: *The Fashionable Tragedian,* 1877, written in collaboration with Archer's close friend and frequent literary partner, R. W. Lowe, the first, most famous, and funniest of the attacks upon Irving's physical and vocal eccentricities, and *Henry Irving, Actor and Manager: A Critical Study*, 1883, a sober and serious piece of criticism. The journalistic work of various kinds was done for *The Edinburgh Evening News*; none of it was ever reprinted, but Charles Archer makes considerable reference to it. At least one of the early plays, *Rosalind*, a two-act comedy, was produced early in 1878 by an Edinburgh amateur group. None of them was published. Late in life, Archer, as Shaw long before him many times had done, disproved the old adage that critics cannot write good plays by his *Green Goddess*, a sensational melo-drama which scored a great success in America and repeated it in England in 1923 with George Arliss as the Raja of Rukh.

The passage beginning after the Archer references and climaxing with the delightful "NEVER TAKE ANYBODY'S ADVICE" is particularly interesting as a summary of Shaw's own early training and discipline. Shaw never tired of expressing his enormous debt to the British Museum reading room; it was there, incidentally, that Archer first discovered him, studying simultaneously Karl Marx and the orchestral score of *Tristan und Isolde*.

The "new play" in process was, of course, *Candida*. Unfortunately Janet Achurch, an emotional and unusually gifted actress whose praises Shaw constantly sang, except for a brief and unsuc-cessful appearance in London in 1900, played the leading role only in the provinces, opening in Aberdeen in 1897. I say unfortunately, because she alone of professional actresses seems to have played Candida Morell as the hypocritical Philistine that Shaw intended her to be. Janet Achurch's husband, Charles Charrington, played Morell; the talented Shakespearean and Ibsenite actor Courtney Thorpe, another of Shaw's favorites, was Marchbanks in the prov-inces; Granville-Barker, who was to repeat the part at the opening of the Barker-Vedrenne-Shaw campaign at the Court in 1904, played Marchbanks in London in 1900. Shaw generously persuaded the Charringtons to engage Ellen Terry's daughter, Edith Craig, as Prossy. When Richard Mansfield was preparing his American production, Shaw managed to sell him the idea of importing Janet Achurch, but her intensity in acting and her desire to play Candida on Shaw's terms (the "quite a sentimental play" is exquisite Shavian irony) as a cold, self-seeking egoist terrified the rather timid and "genteel" Mansfield and he broke the contract.

The Philanderer, a satire on pseudo-Ibsenites, though written in 1893, was turned down by Grein for the Independent Theatre Society, and had to wait until February 1907 for a public performance at the Court Theatre. Despite a strong cast, it was already out-dated, and did not succeed. I was surprised to note that in the summer of 1954 it was revived on the New England "straw-hat" and "citronella" circuit. . . . Sydney Grundy was next in favor to Pinero and Henry Arthur Jones as chief purveyors to the fashionable actor-managers of the nineties of tailor-made vehicles, frequently politely "modern." The reference to his discovery of the New Woman is a near-pun; a play by Grundy with that title had been presented by Fred Terry at the Comedy Theatre early in September. Grundy worked particularly for John Hare, for whom he wrote in 1890 *A Pair of Spectacles,* one of Hare's greatest successes and the only play by Grundy which is at all remembered today. Shaw was to begin his critical career on *The Saturday Review* a month after writing the above letter, January 5, 1895, with a notice of Hare's production of Grundy's *Slaves of the Ring.* . . . Archer, after making Shaw's acquaintance, got him a job on the reviewing staff of *The Pall Mall Gazette* in 1885, under the editorship of the puritanical reformer, W. T. Stead. I assume the "celebrated letter" referred to is one which Shaw wrote to his editor when the latter decided to attack all actresses as immoral, and Shaw in a beautifully ironic vein wrote him a chiding letter, quoted in part in Pearson's biography, pp. 87-88. At least the subject jibes with the point of view expressed in *Mrs. Warren's Profession.*

We have mentioned the first London production of *Arms and the Man,* which brought Bernard Shaw and Golding Bright together. Richard Mansfield produced the play at the Herald Square Theatre in New York on September 17, 1894, and scored a great success as Bluntschli. *Mrs. Warren's Profession* was turned down finally by the shocked Grein and was not produced until 1902, when the Stage Society gave it two performances. We shall encounter later a series of letters written late in 1901 concerning this eventual production. Arnold Daly, a more staunch Shaw champion than Richard Mansfield, produced *Mrs. Warren's Profession* in America in 1905, and it created a *succès de scandale* by being stopped by the police. Daly and his leading lady, Mary Shaw (no relation), were later completely exonerated by the judge who tried the case, but unhappily the play, a serious attack upon organized prostitution, became notorious as a pornographic work (see post-card to M. Marcel Boulestin, dated December 5, 1905, below), and has never received the success it deserved. It is today somewhat dated, and it is early Shaw. But it foreshadows frequently the great playwright to come, and it merits more and more serious revivals than it has attained. If *The Philanderer* had been accepted by Charles Wyndham, the suave and polished high comedian and actor-manager of the Criterion Theatre at the time of writing, it might, with him and his company and his lavish style of production, have succeeded. Jones's *The Case of Rebellious Susan* opened at the Criterion on October 3, 1894, and was a great success. Unhappily, whatever the merits of Shaw's play, there surely *was* no other actor who could "philander as well as Wyndham." Concerning Shaw's promise to himself, if we look forward to the letter of June 10, 1896, we shall find that a month ahead of his own deadline he had finished his *seventh* play.

Obviously, in addition to doing full-dress reviews like that which follows, Bright was now doing regular paragraphing or gossip-column work.

"Odette" at the Princess's

When a *man* (crossed out and "stage hero" substituted by Shaw) discovers firstly a Russian Prince creeping about his drawing-room at midnight, and secondly, his wife in undress standing at her bedroom door, whispering her lover's name, what course shall he pursue? *A passionate Frenchman would kill the wife and fight her seducer, whilst the more phlegmatic Englishman would seek redress in the Divorce Court.* (Crossed out by Shaw, and the following substituted: "If a Frenchman, he must kill his wife and fight her seducer. If an Englishman, he is permitted to seek redress in the Divorce Court.") *Lord Henry Trevene, however, elected to do neither.* (Crossed out by Shaw, and the following witty paraphrase substituted: "Lord Henry Trevene, being in the impossible position of a French stage hero translated into English, finds both these plain paths of duty barred to him.") Accordingly, he denies the justice of a law which unties the nuptial knot only as a preliminary to uniting the guilty lovers. He can see full well what his own future will be—a hopeless blank. So be it! But Odette's life shall be no better. His wife she shall remain till the end, though he will no longer tolerate her presence under the same roof. Go she must and that very night, whilst he will retain their only child, an infant daughter.

Fifteen years elapse, the child Eva has developed into a charming girl of eighteen summers, who knows nothing of the past, but has been taught to believe her mother dead. Eva is engaged to Lord Shandon, and the only bar to their mutual happiness is his mother's sanction, which can be gained by a promise from Odette never to call herself by her married name again, and never to set foot either in Paris or London. At Nice, where all the parties are stopping, Lord Henry sends an ambassador in the person of Philip Eden to induce his wife to consent to these terms. She has sunk low enough in all conscience, living in an establishment that is neither more nor less than a gambling hell kept by an American quack doctor, who never loses at cards. (Here the underlining of the first clause is clear from the letter—Shaw objected to the moral attitude expressed; what his objection was to *loses* is not clear.) In debt, in difficulties, she none the less refuses the proposal of an increased allowance on such conditions. "Sweet is revenge, especially to women." It's her turn now, and she means to make the most of it; she demands to see her child for whom her maternal instinct, though dormant, is yet alive. To this proposition, Lord Henry very weakly consents, provided that she does not reveal her identity. The interview between mother and daughter takes place, when Odette strives to awaken her child's memory to herself, and failing, leaves husband and child alone once more.

Mr. Clement Scott has been pleased to designate this a problem play, thereby seeking to prove that long before "The Second Mrs. Tanqueray" was produced, London had dealt with the subject. *Frankly, I cannot see where the problem comes in, but then I am possibly dense. Dumas fils solved the enigma with the famous 'Tue-la' of La Femme de Claude. In England, a divorce suit would have obviated all the difficulties arising from Lord Henry's silly and altogether inexplicable behaviour.* (The three sentences deleted by Shaw, and the following substituted: "But then every play that touches real life at all is a problem play. The only question that interests us is whether it is a "solution-of-the-problem" play. And will anyone seriously contend that the course taken by Lord Henry is a solution of the problem of how to deal with an unfaithful wife. The famous 'Tue-la' of Dumas fils is reasonable in comparison, and our own divorce court appears a quite divinely wise institution beside the silliness of Lord Henry." After which, obviously pleased with his improvements, Shaw commented: "Here, having disposed of the problem business, you must start a new paragraph, criticising the play as a play solely.") It appears to me that Sardou blundered not once but many times in the construction of his play. (Shaw's comment: "And you mustn't tell a man like Sardou that it appears to you that he has blundered: you must point out what you object to & why you object to it.") It may be that, as it was written some fifteen years ago, and produced in England under the Bancroft régime in '82, it appears stilted and old-fashioned in thought and idea; but under no circumstances can it be called a great play. (Underlining here by Shaw. His comment: "It does not pretend to be a great play. The remark is equally true of Box & Cox, which is nevertheless a very good farce. The question is, is Odette a good play of its class, and what you mean is that it isn't.") One feels instinctively that Sardou got "no forrader," *whereas Mr. Pinero with "The Second Mrs. Tanqueray" really handles a dangerous theme most delicately & infused a strain of genius into his work.* (Foregoing italicized passage crossed out by Shaw. His comment: "You must make an oath never to mention Mrs. Tanqueray again, or even think of her. The one chief and damning disability of the young critic is that he always has some pet author and pet work for whose supremacy he is mortally jealous. He becomes a knight errant indicating the superiority of his Dulcinea over all other ladies. Mrs. Tanqueray is your Dulcinea; and you will never be worth a guinea a column until you grow out of her.")

When Mrs. Anna Ruppert made her début as Camille some four months since, she won the good opinion of Mr. Clement Scott, who informed his readers that the lady *had* (crossed out by Shaw and "possessed" substituted) every quality needed for a successful stage-career. *I do not for one moment wish to set myself up* (Foregoing italicized passage crossed out by Shaw. His comment: "Yes, you do wish to set yourself up, and you are going to do it in the next line. Why shouldn't you? Why deliberately say what you don't mean?") against so distinguished a critic, but I am quite unable to side with him on this point. *"I must be cruel only to be kind"* (This italicized passage, referred to in the letter as an example of taking a moral attitude, received this comment from Shaw in the manuscript —it *was* a *manuscript*, not a typed notice, which Bright sent him: "Never say a thing like this. There is nothing more offensive to artists—and rightly so—than to make a show of sparing their feelings. It is right to be considerate, but horribly wrong to show it") *and when I state that so far as I could discover Mrs. Ruppert showed no sign even of latent talent, it must not be assumed that I am making the lady the subject of a critical attack.* (This longish passage was crossed out by Shaw; his comment: "This unnecessary & self-conscious exculpation is awful. The public is supposed to understand a critic's position without being told.") *Au contraire,* (Crossed out, with eloquent absence of comment, by Shaw) I admire her pluck in attempting to make a success out of a play which with the alluring personality of Modjeska failed to attract. But Mrs. Ruppert is unfortunately not an actress at all. Her performance was amateurish to a fault. *She has not learned the first principles of acting,* (Crossed out by Shaw. His comment: "You mustn't talk about first principles: they don't exist. Poor Mrs. R had been drilled to within an inch of her life in 'the principles' of elocution") nor can she even tread the stage with dignity. Her voice is hard, unsympathetic and monotonous, (Shaw's comment: "Now we are coming to something sensible. You are quite entitled to describe her voice: that is quite a different thing to talking about 'the principles of elocution & acting'") and her *tragic* (Crossed out by Shaw) pathos is deliciously comic. She no more realized the light and shade of Odette's nature than would a schoolgirl appreciate the hidden beauty and poetry of Ophelia or the *sublime tragedy of Mrs. Tanqueray.* (Crossed out by Shaw. His comment: "No, Reginald, no. Not again.") In taking to the stage, Mrs. Ruppert has clearly mistaken her vocation, *and the sooner she realizes this fact the better it will be for her pocket.* (Foregoing crossed out by Shaw. His comment: "It is no part of a dramatic critic's business to make such a remark, which would have been equally true of a fine actress playing the best sort of dramatic poetry.") If the leading lady be weak, however, the rest of the company certainly are not. One piece of acting stands out most vividly, and may possibly drag the play into the quiet waters of success. The audience, annoyed by the incompetence of the manageress, readily appreciated Mr. Charles Warner's skilful impersonation of Lord Henry. We have been too apt to regard this actor as a breezy hero of melodrama only, but last night Mr. Warner proved how mistaken we all were, by playing this trying and difficult part, which is almost wholly in one key, to perfection. (Last word underlined by Shaw. His comment: "Rather strong, eh? It leaves no room for Salvini, or Irving.") *Undoubtedly* (Crossed out by Shaw. His comment: "'Undoubtedly' is not the right way to put it. Many other critics doubted it and ridiculed it. You mean that it *seemed to you* one of the finest &c &c —") it is one of the very finest things he has ever done, worthy of a place next his hauntingly terrible Coupeau. Here and there, perchance, one could detect a false *emphasis* (Crossed out by Shaw, and "note" substituted), a misplaced emphasis; but the whole was so excellent, and <u>played with so firm a grip and manly (never degenerating to maudlin) pathos, that such slight excrescences may readily</u> be condoned. (Underlining by Shaw. His comment: "Now here you are saying something definite—you are writing criticism—you are <u>describing</u> what you saw. Don't you feel how much better it is than mere pompous and unmeaning phrase slinging like 'Undoubtedly it is one of the finest things he has done &c'?") Scarcely less deserving of praise was the cynic Johnny Stratford, sustained with rare skill (Shaw's comment: "This is all right—quite presentable.") and a keen eye for artistic effect by Mr. Bernard Gould. Quite adequate too were Miss Ettie Williams as the *ingénue,* and Mr. Herbert Flemming as Philip Eden. If only Mrs. Ruppert the manageress will induce Mrs. Ruppert, the would-be actress to retire in favour of some one else more fitted for the part, there might perhaps be a long lease in store for this so-called "problem" play.

R. E. G. B.

The production of Sardou's play discussed in Bright's review above ran from September 9 through October 13. William Archer, in his review in *The World* on October 3, 1894, was far more harsh than the budding critic. . . . Clement Scott of *The Daily Telegraph* prided himself as dramatic critic on being the *vox populi;* he had a tremendous photographic memory and could describe accurately what he saw and heard in performance, but he had absolutely no critical judgment or philosophical principles. The resolute enemy of anything new (except the tame actors of "the new school"), he opposed all those things for which Archer of *The World*, Walkley of *The Times*, and finally Shaw of *The Saturday Review* and his successor Max Beerbohm fought most staunchly. Today he is remembered only by scholars of the period. As dramatic critic Shaw attacked him frequently, tauntingly, and delightedly, but the non-intellectual masses of his time contentedly continued their devotion to him and their indifference to Shaw and his group. . . . "The famous 'Tue-la' of Dumas fils" refers to a sentence toward the end of a small volume, *L'Homme-femme*, 1872, Dumas's contribution to a controversy concerning the proper treatment of an adulteress. The sentence, in one translation, reads: "She [the adulteress] is not Woman, she is not even *a* woman; she is not within divine conception; she is purely animal; she is the animal woman of the land of Nod, she is the female of Cain;—kill her." Dumas *fils* almost immediately dramatized his passionate opinion in *La Femme de Claude*, produced in January, 1873, in which, the moment Claude has full proof of his wife's infidelity, he kills her with a new rifle invented by his protegé and her paramour, and turns to the latter with the remark: "And you, come back to work." (For what it is worth—and I submit that it is not in any sense plagiarism, but mere coincidence or unconscious memory—in his fourth dramatic notice, "The Independent Theatre," January 26, 1895, Shaw, writing of Dorothy Leighton's *Thyrza Fleming*, a dramatic "counterblast" to Sarah Grand's *Heavenly Twins*, wrote: "It is exactly as if Shakespeare had written Othello as a confutation of the Tue-la of Dumas *fils*.") . . . *Odette* had first been presented in England during the Bancroft régime at the Haymarket on April 25, 1882, with the famous Polish-born popular emotional favorite of the American stage, Madame Modjeska, in the title role. . . . *Box and Cox*, a wildly impossible and hilarious farce, is probably the only work of the once popular J. Madison Morton now remembered, but, as Professor Ashley H. Thorndike put it, even it "no longer convulses us as it did Queen Victoria." . . . Shaw's very understandable annoyance with the otherwise critically acclaimed *Second Mrs. Tanqueray* he could not express at length at the time of production since he was then a music critic, but in his eighth *Saturday Review* column, February 22, 1895, he took the occasion of the publication of the play as an excuse for an hilarious but beautifully trenchant analysis of its real weaknesses. (*Our Theatres in the Nineties*, I.44-48.) ... Mrs. Anna Ruppert seems to have been one of several usually wealthy socialite amateurs of the nineties who with no particular training or talent audaciously courted audience and critical disapproval by assembling casts of professionals and attempting to hold among and against them the center of the stage. Archer's attempt to be "considerate" in his criticism of her as Odette is amusing: he conceded her a fair intelligence and "a certain amount of force and feeling," but slyly noted her sad handicap, "the extreme exiguity of her physique." Later in the same month of October, 1894, following her failure in the Sardou vehicle, she heroically appeared in a fantastic melodrama of the Australian bushrangers called *Robbery under Arms* and by "equestrian feats" on-stage terrified poor Archer, who nevertheless decided she was a better horsewoman than a Sardou adulteress. ... Charles Warner, a powerful emotional actor possessed of gusto and electrical quality, suffered considerably from the bread-and-butter necessity of appearing almost solely in the teacup-and-saucer roles of the "new school," pseudo-realistic, Robertsonian drama. His one really sensational success was scored at the Princess's in 1879 as the hero Coupeau in Charles Reade's dramatization of Zola's *Drink*; here his naturalistically detailed death-struggles in a fit of *delirium tremens* were compared with Henry Irving's varied and famous melodramatic death scenes. ... Bernard Gould had appeared, we have noted, as Sergius in Shaw's *Arms and the Man.*

4. More Practical Advice to the Young Journalist, with Shavian Examples

29 Fitzroy Square W.
14th Dec., 1894.

Dear Sir,

The paragraph does not refer to "Mrs. Warren's Profession", which has not yet been submitted to the Censor. I do not know what it refers to. It sounds like Henry James & Alexander; but I have heard nothing about it.

This year license was refused by Mr. Pigott to a play by Mr. Sidney Olivier, who, as an upper division clerk in the Colonial Office, ranks as a more highly qualified man than Mr. Pigott, whose appointment is a matter of patronage, and who might quite possibly be an illiterate person, whereas an upper division civil servant has to pass a very stiff examination. The License was applied for by Miss Farr, who wished to produce the play at the Avenue Theatre. Mr. Olivier attempted to discuss the question with Mr. Pigott, but found him to be an ignorant and prejudiced opponent of the movement begun by Ibsen. It was quite useless to talk to him; he was well intentioned enough, but incapable. This is the only recent example of Censorial despotism with which I am acquainted.

Do not write a book with the purpose of burning it. Write it on the assumption that it is going to be published and to be useful and successful. Then see what will happen. Probably you will be unable to find a publisher; and you will have learnt so much by the effort of writing that you will go on afresh & pass it by. But don't burn it, even if you become ashamed of it. Keep it in a drawer somewhere. At thirty, you will be impatient of the stuff you wrote at twenty; but at forty, you will recover some of your respect for the dreams of youth. Besides, it may turn out worth publishing. One never knows. The one certain thing is you must write, write, write every day for several years if you are to become a master workman in your profession.

As to your suggestion that perhaps I was better able to afford such exercises than you, I can only say that the difference between us appears to be that your father is fairly well off, whereas mine was poor and embarrassed. If your board and lodging are guaranteed, you may consider yourself a king. If you had seen me about twelve years ago, you would have seen a grimly shabby figure. For about nine years after I came to London I made nothing & wrote a good deal. Then for five or six years I made about £150. Then for a few years I made nearly

£300. At present my income has gone back to its old figure—0. So you see money does not matter so much. A prosperous stock-broker would consider my career a dismal one; but as a matter of fact if you consider the variety of my interests and activities, the friends I have made (not to mention the enemies), the consideration I enjoy, and the degree of personal efficiency I have acquired, you will, I think, see that if I had devoted myself to making several thousand a year as a stockbroker, I should have ,made a very bad bargain. And remember that I began as much handicapped by poverty, shyness, awkwardness, and all the miseries of weak immaturity as anybody could have done. You have probably twice my opportunities & advantages, if not ten times. The fact is that everybody has to stand the same racket more or less—more if he is penniless, less if he has a father who guarantees a roof and a meal. So go ahead: the world's your oyster.

G. B. S.

It is impossible to identify, at this date and place, the "paragraph" referred to, or its content. The linking of the names of Henry James and the actor-manager George Alexander obviously refers to Shaw's belief that the point lay in Alexander's preparation for James's *Guy Domville*, which was to be produced at the St. James's on January 5, 1895. (With Wilde's *An Ideal Husband* it formed the subject of Shaw's second *Saturday Review* article.) This play scored—James's, of course, not Wilde's—an historic failure which drove from Henry's mind his long cherished ambition to become a playwright and turned him back into his prose fiction, eventually to write his three masterpieces.

E. F. Smyth Pigott was for twenty years examiner and therefore Censor of plays under the Lord Chamberlain, and his squeamish, puritanical, and sometimes apparently almost whimsical judgments had long offended playwrights and critics. In his fourth dramatic notice of the next month, *à propos* (a phrase that would probably have been deleted by Shaw) the publication of William

Heinemann's *The First Step,* to which Pigott had refused a license, Shaw referred publicly to the similar refusal accorded his good friend and fellow-Fabian Sidney Olivier's *A Freedom in Fetters.* About a month later Pigott died rather suddenly and Shaw devoted his March 1st column to a consideration of his work as Censor and the whole question of censorship, which was to remain a personal hazard in his own career for so many years to come. Refusing, as Clement Scott had done, to observe the old advice *de mortuis nil nisi boni* as applying to obituaries on Pigott, Shaw (*Our Theatres in the Nineties,* I.48-55) searchingly and scarifyingly summed up all the stupidities and indignities committed by Pigott and under his censorial rule, and asked that with his passing the Censorship be abolished. . . . Florence Farr, one of Shaw's many actress friends and apparently an intimate one, we have already referred to. It was she whom Miss A. E. F. Horniman subsidized to produce *Arms and the Man.*

Possibly one comment might be made about the paragraph concerning the preservation of early manuscripts. Shaw's novels, except for the last, *An Unsocial Socialist,* were not published, even serially, for some years; but the first, as previously noted, although written in 1879, reached print eventually only in the Standard Edition of 1930.

5. More Practical Advice

29 Fitzroy Square W.
11th Jan. 1895

Dear Sir

The worst of this paragraphing business is that it deals so much with persons and brings you across all manner of personal dislikes and quarrels which cause your work to be thrown aside through no fault of your own. For instance, Runciman, the musical critic of the Saturday, who is perhaps the best of recent editorial finds in the way of a critic, was for a time working for the Sun. They actually dismissed him out of sheer inability to know a good man when they had got hold of him. Being a good man he has character enough to make enemies. So has Frank Harris. So have I. A paragraph about all three of us has several chances against it in any newspaper office in London. As you probably saw, I ran the gauntlet in The Star successfully, though I do not know who the paragraphist was. I think you would do well to invest a few shillings (only three, I think) in a huge volume called Sell's Dictionary of the world's press, Fleet St. near Fetter Lane, and study it carefully with a view to seeing what you could do in the way of manifolding your paragraphs and sending them simultaneously to several papers throughout the country. I have not had experience enough of this sort of journalism to advise you as to details; but it seems to me that this is a thing that an enterprising man ought to do. If you could persuade your father to equip you with a Remington or Worth typewriter (these are the best for such rough handling as manifolding requires) as part of the necessary outfit for a young man desirous of being up to date in an office, you could make at least ten copies of a paragraph with carbon paper, and send them simultaneously to ten different papers in ten different districts, with, of course, a chance of two or three of them being inserted. You could offer a weekly column of theatrical gossip and news at a low price— say ten or fifteen shillings—to a number of papers whose circulations do not overlap, and whose day of publication is the same, and try to make it pay by getting more than one paper to take it. But be careful to see that the proprietors of the papers you approach are different, as there are some provincial newspapers which are practically duplicates issued by the same firm in widely distant parts of the kingdom. Even if you don't succeed, you will pick up a certain knowledge of the press, and you will find out the sort of questions you ought to put to the men who do make this sort of thing pay. It is always worth

while to do a thing the wrong way in order to find out how not
to do it, which is an important step towards finding out how
to do it.

I am much obliged to you for your appreciation of my Saturday articles. In a way your opinion of Grundy's play is fairer
than mine, as you take the thing on its merits, whereas I am
partly fighting against the leading of the drama further in a
direction which I believe to be, for the present, the wrong direction. And I greatly dislike the clumsy device (as it seems
to me) of "the reasoner" introduced to explain the play—the
Thouvenin of Dumas fils. The courage that struck you as to
the ending was discounted for me by two things. First, the
wretched claptrap about "the thin red line", which, as you may
imagine, did not seem very courageous to the author of "Arms
and the Man"; and second, the stupidity of the conclusion that
there is no solution of the difficulty of unhappy marriages,
whereas there is a perfectly simple solution in reform of the divorce laws. In some American States, South Dakota for instance, those four people could have re-sorted themselves quite
easily. It is quite a feature of stageland and the aloofness of our
theatrical people from real life that dramatists are always pro-
pounding as Sphinx-enigmas questions that every practical
man knows the answer to, whilst they skip light-heartedly over
situations which in real life raise the most appalling difficulties.
As to the acting, poor Brandon Thomas of course did what he
could, and did it very well, to pull off the impossible part. I
saw the play on the second night; and Miss Calhoun, though
not bad as far as she went, certainly did not do as much as
might have been done with that one scene which was all that
justified the existence of the play, and was in fact the root of it.
You must not dismiss Gilbert Hare as beneath contempt. Suppose your father bought The World, and handed over the theatrical column to you, you would at first probably disappoint
the readers who were accustomed to Archer's work. But if you
turned out a fairly presentable column, and really did your

blood best, correcting every sentence carefully and taking your work earnestly, all the good men who had been through the mill would admit that you had a right to your trial. If you want to enjoy masterly acting twenty years hence, you must be very tender to the apprentices and journeymen of today.

I doubt if I shall republish my Saturday articles. I never could be persuaded to do so with my World articles. Taken out of the atmosphere of the week in which they were written, they lose half their freshness.

G. B. S.

Shaw was now officially on the staff of Frank Harris's weekly. His fellow critic was John F. Runciman, whose uncle James, a well-known amateur boxer, had been dissuaded by Shaw from his desire to dramatize the Shavian novel about a boxer, *Cashel Byron's Profession.* Again one notes the really personal interest in young Bright's career as the busy Shaw takes time to mention such details as the press-dictionary, the very make of typewriter most useful, and the amount to charge for the gossip-paragraphs. We shall see later how carefully Bright followed Shaw's advice and how much use he made in his column and in paragraphs of information given him by the older critic. The reference to Bright's appreciation of the *Saturday* articles is puzzling, unless he had access to proofs or copies before actual distribution, for the letter is dated January 11th, and Shaw's second review the 12th. We have noted that the first had dealt with Grundy's *Slaves of the Ring*; it sounded immediately one of the themes that Shaw was to pursue for three and a half years, his attack upon the fundamentally petty and piddling drama of the Pinero-Jones-Grundy school. The accepted term for the mouthpiece of the dramatist in the well-made play of pseudo-social impact, which Shaw translated into English, was, and has remained, usually in the French form, the *raisonneur*. Thouvenin was the *raisonneur* in the *Denise* of Dumas *fils*. How arbitrarily the French makers of the "thesis-play" relied upon this usually wooden character is suggested by Dumas' comment in the notes to *Denise:*

"Everything that Thouvenin says is irrefutable." In his review
Shaw was very amusing in his comments on Brandon Thomas, who
played Grundy's *raisonneur,* and who seemed to Shaw to be in "a
deplorable situation throughout." "The thin red line" reference,
with the play not available, cannot be accurately identified, but
the mention of Shaw's anti-militaristic *Arms and the Man* makes
clear that it was a bit of patriotic or jingoistic propaganda about
the conventional last-ditch heroism of the red-coated soldiers of the
Queen. The title of the play, of course, suggests the theme; Grundy
hypothecated the indissolubility of marriages. The play had two
leading ladies, Eleanor Calhoun, a pretty and popular young ingénue, and Kate Rorke, a more trained and competent straight
actress. John Hare, actor-manager, produced *Slaves of the Ring* at
the Garrick; Gilbert Hare, as the context shows, was his son. One
might be baffled by the phrase "blood best," and be tempted to
think the first word a misprint or an anticipation of Liza Doo-
little's later famous "shocker" adjective; but obviously it refers to
the father-son relationship.

One must certainly grant Bright's considerable critical acumen
in perceiving as soon as Shaw began his dramatic criticism that his
articles should be rescued from periodical files. The American critic
James Huneker was responsible for a badly collected and edited
two-volume winnowing of the dramatic criticism in 1906. Shaw
himself edited a complete three-volume collection for the Standard
Edition in 1932, when he also assembled his music criticism (1890–
1894) from *The World* in three volumes. Five years later he did
likewise for a single-volume collection of his 1888–1889 *Star* musical notices. His last sentence might apply to much collected criticism, Clement Scott's for instance, but the best Shavian critics have
constantly insisted that his own musical and dramatic criticism
remains today, well over half-a-century later, eminently readable
even to those who know nothing of the plays or compositions, the
players or performers, discussed.

6. Some Advice to a Puzzled and Unhappy Son (or, How to Live on £50 a Year)

29 Fitzroy Square W.
30th Jan. 1895

Dear Mr. Bright

This is just the sort of case in which children are atrociously cruel to their parents. The first thing to do is to clear your mind of all protests against the position of your father's wife. No matter who or what she is or was, or whether you and your brothers and sisters like or dislike her, your father's claim to be happy with the woman he prefers and to marry her, and put her interests before those of everyone else is indisputable. Of course it is a very disagreeable turn of events for the family, but it is not a grievance. If you take it in bad part, you will do pure, unmitigated, useless harm, since the marriage cannot be undone (even if it were reasonable to demand that it should); and besides, by making your father's relation with his children resentful and miserable, you will throw him more helplessly than ever on the sympathy of his wife, and almost drive him to make an unfair division of his property in her favour when he dies.

£50 a year is a fortune to a man in your position. You can't take hansoms on it, nor patronise the three and sixpenny lunch and the seven and sixpenny table d'hote at the Criterion on it, nor go to the stalls on it, nor live in a Whitehall Court flat on it; but you can keep yourself on it much better than most city clerks can keep a wife and family on it. With such an endowment you haven't the ghost of a claim on your father, though you must bid a long farewell to the style of living indicated by a house in the country and an income of £2,000 a year. I presume the Regent's Park Terrace ménage is beyond your new means; so you better at once look for a cheap room as near the British Museum as you can get it and arrange with the landlady for your breakfast. Then select a cheap restaurant, or study the art of dining cheaply at Gatti's, for instance. Get a ticket for the museum library, and study the drama there up to eight every night with all the advantages of communal heating, lavatory accommodation and electric light, with a comfortable seat, unlimited books, and ink and blotting paper all for nothing. When you are settled in this groove with your necessary expenditure well within the fifty, write to your father, and tell him that he may now cut off the supplies altogether; excuse yourself pleasantly for having perhaps made a little unnecessary friction over the second Mrs Tan—I mean Bright; and wish him every domestic happiness and farewell. By cutting the cable before the supplies are exhausted you will prove that you are not merely making the best of a bad job, but boldly tackling the world as an independent man, in which character your father will not after be able to help respecting you. And I assure you you will write ever so much better after having shewn your mettle to yourself as well as to your father, who will begin to value you the moment you are able to do without him, possibly with favourable effects on his will, though I need hardly say that a calculation on that need not trouble a man of your years.

Excuse my giving you good advice: I have no doubt you get plenty of it. But what can I say on the case, as you put it to me, but what I have said?

You are really too hard on Wilde. His "I have enjoyed myself very much" was an Irishman's way of giving all the credit to the actors and effacing his own claims as author.

All the paragraphs about Alexander having accepted a piece

of mine are wrong. The only correct statement of the case is that in this week's World.

yours sincerely
G. Bernard Shaw.

The unknown youth who had booed Shaw in April, 1894, had indeed in less than a year become dependent upon the critic-playwright as confidant, guide, and counselor, even in family matters. The letter is self-explanatory. But note Shaw's emphasis, again and in detail, upon the usefulness of his beloved British Museum. "Mrs Tan—," of course, refers to that character in the Pinero play who he claimed was Bright's Dulcinea and who was for a long time his own *bête noire*. One doubts he actually made a slip of the pen; more probably it is an attempt to introduce a light note into a rather embarrassing letter; remember Shaw had not yet even met his correspondent and so could know only *of* the latter's family. Wilde's enigmatic and "Irish" comment referred to Charles Hawtrey's production of *An Ideal Husband* at the Haymarket, January 3, 1895. I cannot check the comment on Alexander and a Shaw "piece" in *The World*, but suspect it had reference to the actor-manager's offer to play Marchbanks in *Candida* if Shaw would make him blind as a bid for audience-sympathy. This remark is almost as obtuse as the American Richard Mansfield's upon the same play and part. (See a letter from him to Shaw in an article by F. E. Loewenstein in *Drama* for Autumn, 1946.)

7. Extended Comment on the Shaw-Bright Controversy over Paula Tanqueray

29 Fitzroy Square W.
22nd April 1895.

Dear Mr. Bright

As usual my letters have been standing over unanswered for a long time; and I am later than I intended to be in con-

gratulating you on having so promptly and energetically faced
and dealt with the situation created by your father's action.
To tell you the truth I was curious to see whether you would
have stuff enough in you to tackle it; for though it seems a simple matter enough, yet with a great many men—especially men
of the artistic and literary temperament—a call for action ends
like the first scene of the third act of Peer Gynt, where Peer
sees the man chop his finger off to escape from military service.

> "Ay, think of it—wish it done—will it to boot—
> But do it—! No, that's past my understanding!"

I congratulate you especially on the fact that all your friends
and relations regard you as a madman. That is an indispensable
beginning to a respectable, independent life.

In your first letter you express yourself as rather staggered
by my statement that a woman like Paula Tanqueray is the
same at three as at thirty-three. That, however, is quite true.
Rousseau dates his sensual susceptibility "from his birth", three
years earlier than I have allowed for Paula. And there is no
question of her being "corrupt, immoral in thought and idea":
that is begging the whole question of morality. She is different
from Ellean; but so is a poet different from a mathematician.
If you take the mathematician's temperament as a moral standard, of course the poet stands condemned; but why should
you? If you take Ellean as the standard, Paula is condemned;
but again, why not take Paula as the standard, and condemn
Ellean as cold, unnatural, selfish and so on (which is what the
Paula sort of woman invariably does)? A critic must not take
sides in this way without very careful consideration; for it
takes all sorts to make a world; and if you could make every
woman a Saint Elizabeth, the result would be practically as
disastrous as if you made every woman a Catherine II.

Your defence of Paula will not, I think, hold water. Let me
remind you of it, by the way, as you have probably forgotten
it by this time. You say, "She was, so far as study and observation can teach me, (not bad. Master Reginald, for a pure effort

of your imagination) the daughter of a well-to-do, respectable man, probably a dignitary of the church. Chance threw her into the company of a fast set; and moral ruin followed slowly but surely—facilis descensus Averni". But why did she join the fast set? We are all thrown into the company of fast sets. We are all thrown into the company of slow sets too, and of religious sets, and political sets, and fashionable sets, and sporting sets, and gambling sets, and hideously debauched sets. But none of them rush at us and enlist us by a press-gang. We have to seek them out, to shew our sympathy with them, to make ourselves congenial company for them, before we can get into them. If Paula was the daughter of a dignitary of the church, it must have been far easier for her to become a district visitor or half a dozen other respectable things than a prostitute. Why then did she become a prostitute? Because she was built that way, and for no other reason. I dare say your father is at this moment sorrowfully explaining to some friend that you were as sensible as possible at seventeen, and that you were well started at a city office, but that you unfortunately got into a set of theatrical loafers called the Playgoers' Club, and that they seduced you from the paths of business and corrupted you slowly but surely, and so on. But you know very well that the Playgoers' Club didn't come to you: you went to it because you are built that way, just as Paula went off in Mr. Jarman's yacht instead of going into Ellean's convent, which was presumably equally within her reach. It is true that the whole female sex is driven towards prostitution or towards marriage for money (which is the same thing) by economic pressure which, in the case of very poor women, is almost irresistible; but that does not account for the difference between one woman and another in such matters, though it accounts for some of the difference between a man and a woman.

A remark of yours about the difficulties of indulging in a Saturday Review at a cost of sixpence a week suggests to me that you have not realised the advantages of Communism yet. At the Charing Cross end of St. Martin's Lane you will find a free library, with a newspaper room in the basement. You have nothing to do but walk in and read all the papers without any formality whatsover; and when you are done, you can go to the floor above and read all the magazines. We are trying to get a library for St. Pancras; but we were beaten at the last poll. With the British Museum reading room around the corner, and this library within twelve minutes walk, you are five hundred a year richer than Shakespeare.

I cannot bring myself to republish my articles. They appear very entertaining in the context of the events of the week in which they appear; but just because they are good journalism, they are bad literature. I don't think the actress-manageress is going to do much good, because, obviously, she will want plays with good parts for the woman and bad parts for the men; and so, though we shall have two sorts of bad plays instead of one—the actress-manageress's play at half the theatres and the actor-manager's play at the other half, we shall be as far as ever from the genuine drama. My preface is not an advocacy of the changes which I see coming, but simply a statement of them.

I shall go at Grein about the throwing open of the gallery at the I. T. If they really do that, it is a scandalous affair. Probably the truth is that the doorkeepers neglect their business and desert their posts.

yours sincerely,

G. B. S.

First, it is obvious that Bright had written at least twice to Shaw before G. B. S. got around to this reply. Hence the "first letter" in the first sentence of the second paragraph does not refer to the beginning of the correspondence a year before, but to a letter of Bright's written after Shaw's last, but as yet unanswered. . . . *Peer Gynt* is, of course, Ibsen's great play about the magnificent boaster and egoist who rounds the world in weird and incredible adventures in search of himself to return finally after many years to the wife who alone knew him and so could give him back to himself. . . . Shaw's remark concerning Paula Tanqueray, that "a woman of that sort is already the same at three as she is at thirty-three," occurred in his column of February 23, 1895, already referred to. Ellean was Aubrey Tanqueray's daughter by his first wife; many critics or readers of the play today (definitely not representative of "the Paula sort of woman") would unhesitatingly condemn her as "cold, unnatural, selfish and so on." Although Bright was to use only his third name and his surname, the R., as we noted in Shaw's editing of the *Odette* review, stood for Reginald. Considerable and long acquaintance with Pinero's over-rated play leaves me completely baffled as to why Reginald—or Golding—should have imagined Paula's father "a dignitary of the church." Ellean's mother had been a cold and rigid Roman Catholic who, failing to understand Aubrey, had placed the child first in a French and then in an Irish convent. . . . Note again Shaw's knowledge of where and how to get a free education. St. Pancras was the vestry in which Shaw lived and was active politically throughout the nineties. The sections of London now called boroughs were known as vestries until the early 1900's. Shaw eventually served as a vestryman (1897–1900) and a borough councilman (1900–1903), the same position really, and equivalent pretty much to that of an American alderman. . . . With reference to his comments upon republishing his criticisms, it is worth noting again that Shaw was later to change his mind completely concerning journalism in literature and vehemently and repeatedly to pride himself, I think justly, upon achieving his finest results in all his writings by *being* a good journalist. . . . The actress-manageress discussion refers to the concluding portion of a twenty-page preface which had introduced the recently published *Theatrical 'World' of 1894*, the second of five annual volumes collecting William Archer's dramatic criticisms from *The World*. The I. T. of the last paragraph stands for The Independent Theatre, Ltd. (as Grein's enterprise had been renamed), and the gallery must have been thrown open during the group's sponsoring of Lugné-Poë's Théâtre de L'Œuvre in late March and early April in a repertoire of two Ibsen and two Maeterlinck plays.

8. On *Mrs. Warren's Profession*

---

29 Fitzroy Square W.
4th Novr. 1895.

Dear Sir

Will you excuse an answer scribbled in a metropolitan train. The paragraph you send me is (from its point of view) accurate enough. The actress alluded to is Mrs. Theodore Wright, to whom I proposed the part of Mrs. Warren. She was greatly startled when I read it to her; but the suggestion that she considered it a play that ought not to have been written will, I hope, be met presently by the announcement that she has consented to play the part. She has not done so yet, because she is only acquainted with the first two acts (an accidental visitor interrupted my reading of it to her); but she is at any rate quite open to consider it.

The play is a cold bloodedly appalling one; but not in the least a prurient one. Mrs. Warren is much worse than a prostitute. She is an organism of prostitution—a woman who owns and manages brothels in every big city in Europe and is proud of it. With her gains she has had her daughter highly educated and respectably brought up in complete ignorance of the source of her mother's income. The drama of course, lies in the discovery and its consequences. These consequences, though cruel enough, are all quite sensible and sober, no suicide nor sensational tragedy of any sort. Nobody's conscience is smitten except, I hope, the conscience of the audience. My intention is that they shall go home thoroughly uncomfortable. I can at least guarantee that any person who goes to gratify any prurient curiosity will be completely disappointed, as I am not a pandar posing as a moralist. The play has horrified everyone who has heard it, but only as an honest treatment of such a subject ought to horrify them. I want to make an end, if I can, of the furtively lascivious Pharisaism of stage immorality, by a salutary demonstration of the reality. Miss Janet Achurch at once offered to play the part of the daughter, in whom I have sought to put on the stage for the first time (as far as I know) the highly educated, capable, independent young woman of the governing class as we know her today, working, smoking, preferring the society of men to that of women simply because men talk about the questions that interest her and not about servants and babies, making no pretence of caring much about art or romance, respectable through sheer usefulness & strength, and playing the part of the charming woman only as the amusement of her life, not as the serious occupation. What do you think of that as a program for a heroine? To soften the prospect I may add that her lover will be a youth of infinite charm, absolutely good-for-nothing, and absolutely pleasant. The Independent Theatre will find no difficulty in filling the parts. If the play were as vile as has been suggested, neither Miss Achurch or any other artist would touch it. Why should they, since it could do them nothing but harm?

It may interest you to know that although I had little leisure during my autumn holiday in South Wales with the Sidney Webbs, I managed to complete a one act play the hero of which is Napoleon Buonaparte—the Napoleon of the first Italian campaign, aged 27. The other characters are a strange lady, a sub-lieutenant, and an innkeeper; and the whole is in the high comedy vein of "Arms and the Man." I have made no attempt to get it produced, as my position as dramatic critic makes it very difficult for me to take the initiative in any negotiation with our managers.

You can use all this information at your discretion, except that Mrs. Theodore Wright's name must be kept back until she has actually consented to play Mrs. Warren. Make an interview of it if you like, though I should like a peep at it before it goes to press in that case, as I am writing in haste without much consideration.

If you want to know anything about me at any time, don't hesitate to ask. I hope your plucky start has turned out well.

yrs sincerely
G. Bernard Shaw.

Shaw was always a great conserver of time, but especially during the busy days of the nineties he seems to have made almost a habit of writing on metropolitan trains, even to putting into the pocket-notebooks he always carried shorthand passages for the plays. . . . Mrs. Theodore Wright, who had played Mrs. Alving in the now famous first Independent Theatre production and who was to repeat the part for three performances in 1897, was a well-known amateur who, as Shaw once put it, had "played Shakespeare and recited Shelley, Hood, and George Eliot before Karl Marx, Morris, Bradlaugh, and other volcanic makers of the difference between 1837 and 1897." From the time of her first appearance in *Ghosts,* she made occasional short excursions into professional productions, usually with the Independent Theatre, always to critical and audience acclaim, but she never followed the stage as a regular career. Had not *Mrs. Warren's Profession* met insurmountable difficulties of production for so long, she probably would have played it, and her performance, one judges from the records of her other parts, especially if coupled with the Vivie of Janet Achurch, might well have removed from the play the charges of pruriency which prevented for so long an appreciation of its actual and not inconsiderable virtues. As things turned out, the misunderstandings of the point and purpose of Shaw's attack continued for years, evidences of it appearing later in this correspondence. Unfortunately Shaw's opinion of the play expressed here proved entirely unjustified. . . . The one-act play concerning Napoleon was *The Man of Destiny*, of which we shall shortly hear much from Shaw. His integrity as a critic, always a first principle with him, was never so strongly evidenced as in his constant refusal to accept any favors from managers, especially the actor-managers. Archer and Walkley, here as on so many points, agreed with him, but it had for long been an accepted *quid pro quo* arrangement between many critics and managers that the latter take options on plays written by critics which they had no intention of producing, in return for favorable notices of productions, regardless of what the critics might actually think of them. Shaw's almost casual permission to Bright to "make an interview" at once shows his confidence in the young man whom he had not yet even met and foreshadows his own fairly regular—and frequently highly entertaining—habit of writing interviews with himself.

9. What a Young Critic Should Read

29 Fitzroy Sqr. W.
11th Novr. 1895.

Dear Sir

I must content myself with a hasty line. It is very possible that the Licenser will object to "Mrs. Warren's Profession". It is not as yet settled whether the I. T. will give an invitation performance of the play without troubling him (as was done in the case of "Ghosts") or apply for a license & risk the dropping of the project through his refusal. Until this be settled, I think the point had better not be raised. The date is not fixed; but "Mrs. Warren's Profession" will come *after* "Little Eyolf", not before it.

All this overtime in the city is very objectionable from the point of view of health as well as leisure. For the moment I see no escape except by getting another berth, or some journalistic work.

As to what to read, read anything you feel curious about. It's quite possible that your real interest may not lie in the theatre at all. But in any case, read dramatic literature, not histories or criticisms of it. Read three or four of the most famous plays of Molière & Victor Hugo; and sample Beaumarchais, Voltaire, De Musset, Augier, & Dumas fils until you know their styles. Read all Goethe's plays & a lot of Schiller's. Read a rhymed play of Dryden's, a play of Wycherley's, some of Congreve's, several of Sheridan, a Boucicault & a Robertson. Read Aeschylus, Sophocles, Euripides & Aristophanes (the Greek literature is very short). Get translations if you don't know the languages. Read them with a notion of their chronological order. Read Ibsen all through. Also Cibber's Apology & any memoirs of actors that you can unearth. That will do for a beginning. If you meet me anywhere, introduce yourself to me, if you don't mind. In haste.

G. Bernard Shaw.

Shaw's optimism of the previous week was already dampened; George Alexander Redford, successor to the late and (at least by Shaw) unlamented Pigott as Censor of Plays, proved, if anything, more rigid than his predecessor, and Shaw was to have years of personal, rather than mainly disinterested as with Pigott, war with him. Not only, however, was *Mrs. Warren's Profession* held up indefinitely by the stupid and senseless bonds and moral codes of the nineties, but the *Little Eyolf* of Ibsen had to wait until November 28 of the following year, when it was produced at the Avenue by the American actress and great friend of Henry James, Elizabeth Robins, with Janet Achurch and Mrs. Pat Campbell as co-stars with the manageress.

The last paragraph, however obvious the advice may seem to seasoned and experienced critics and scholars, still contains today, sixty years after Shaw penned it "In haste," a remarkably sound and inspired list of preliminary reading to serve as introduction

to theatre and drama for any interested young person or beginner.
Today, of course, we should add a very few authors of those sixty
years, beginning with "Read most of Shaw." The playwrights
mentioned certainly need no comment. The only actor's memoirs
included by name is the first of its kind in English, the completely
delightful *An Apology for the Life of Mr. Colley Cibber, Comedian*
(1740).

The reader will probably, even though given warning earlier,
come upon the last sentence with a start of distinct surprise; in a
year and a half Shaw had got his young heckler of the *Arms and
the Man* première settled in journalism, he had given him endless
practical and professional advice, he had acted gratuitously but
most meticulously as his editor, he had given him invaluable material to use in his gossip paragraphs, he had persuaded him to leave
the unhappy and uncomfortable parental roof and become independent—*but*—he and young Golding Bright had not yet actually
met in person. The whole relationship here must certainly be
unique, if all the circumstances are considered, in discipleship and
unlimited and undemanding patronage of the arts or those crafts
allied to them.

10. Shaw's Lack of Ill-Feeling about the Failure of the Early Plays to Reach the Professional Stage, and a Review of the History to Date of those Plays

29 Fitzroy Square W.
10th June, 1896.

Dear Bright

No: there's no ring: there never really is. Since "Arms
& The Man" I have written three plays, one of them only a one-
act historical piece about Napoleon. The first of these was

"Candida"; and there are obvious reasons for its not being produced—my insistence on Miss Achurch for the heroine, the fact that the best man's part in it is too young for any of our actor managers (Esmond appears to be the only possible man for it), and the character of the play itself, which is fitter for a dozen select matinées than for the evening bill. The second—the Napoleon piece—has practically never been offered to anybody, because Ellen Terry took a fancy to it, and Irving proposed to produce it and play Napoleon. But I want this kept strictly private, as it may easily come to nothing, like other projects that get talked over and are afterwards crowded out by the march of events. The third play is only just finished. The only manager who has seen it (in rough draft) is Daniel Frohman, who is perfectly friendly & is as likely as not to produce it in New York if we come to terms, whilst there is no backwardness on the part of our managers in wanting to see it. Considering that my plays are difficult, that nobody believes there is much money in them, that even their commonplaces—what you and I would think their commonplaces—strike our managers as curiously novel and advanced, and that all managers like to be courted a little and are perhaps offended by the reticence which my position as critic imposes on me in this respect—not to mention the infuriating effect of my criticisms occasionally: taking all this into account, I have nothing to complain of; indeed the wonder is that they are so attentive and so interested in my attempts. The fact is, the business of a manager is too desperately difficult and hazardous to admit of any trifling with rings or the like. Whatever Wyndham may have said or advised about a play not his own, I have not the slightest doubt that if I brought him a play tomorrow with which he could see his way to even three months' good business, he would jump at it, though it were calculated to send all the inmates of Marlboro' House into convulsions. A manager is kept so desperately sharply to business by the terrible drain of from £500 to £1000 a week going remorselessly on all the time, and his knowledge (derived from bitter experience) of how easily the receipts may drop from £100 a week to practically nothing, that he is forced to consider only what the public wants from him; and if you find him giving them what they don't want, and withholding what they do want, you may always take the straightforward explanation that his judgment is at fault. It is true that in the theatrical profession people are always talking Machiavelli, so to speak, and devising imaginary diplomacies and boycotts and compacts and the deuce knows what not; but at the first whiff of a success in prospect, all that is flung to the winds. The opinion of the Prince of Wales had absolutely no effect on "Arms & The Man". Nothing affected it, not even the cab strike. Every night some twenty or thirty pounds worth of people solemnly walked in and paid their money, the total receipts for the run being £1777 (I always remember it because of the sevens). The cost was probably five or six thousand. The astonishing thing, to an outsider, is that this result, of which no secret has been made, does not really impress managers as being particularly disastrous: theatrical business means making one success pay for half a dozen failures, and the half dozen failures seldom come off as well as "Arms & The Man" when allowance is made for the absence of a regular clientèle such as can always be depended on for a minimum at the Lyceum or Criterion. Wyndham, for instance (who has been very friendly to me), would probably look at it in this way. "If this fellow Shaw can pull in a couple of thousand pounds 'on his own,' and I can always pull in so much on my own, no matter what I play in, and the Criterion can always pull in so much on its own as a theatre with a reputation as a safe place to go to for a jolly evening with people who don't know one author or actor from another, then, next time I run short of safe plays and am forced to risk an experiment, I stand to lose £2000 less, in the worst event, than if I ventured with a quite untried man." But of course as long as he has plays at hand with which he feels quite safe, he will not produce mine, which seem to him to be quarter of a century ahead of the public. So you see there is no more a ring against me than there is against Ibsen or Sudermann. Twenty years ago Grundy complained fiercely that there was a ring, because no manager would touch his plays as long as there was one by Byron to be had, or else the inevitable adaptation from the French. Nowadays no manager will produce one of my plays as long as there is one by Grundy available—or Jones, or Pinero, or Carton &c. Twenty years hence, if I prove a success as a dramatist, nobody will produce a play by a beginner of 1916 as long as there is a play by me on the market. There is no ring—there never is, never has been, never will be, although there always seems to be one to the younger generation battering at the door.

The news about "Mrs. Warren's Profession" is no longer true. There is no question of its immediate or remote production. The facts are rather funny, in a way. My first three plays, "Widowers' Houses," "The Philanderer," and "Mrs. Warren's Profession" were what people would call realistic. They were dramatic pictures of middle class society from the point of view of a Socialist who regards the basis of that society as thoroughly rotten economically and morally. In "Widowers' Houses" you had the rich suburban villa standing on the rents of the foul rookery. In "The Philanderer" you had the fashionable cult of Ibsenism and "New Womanism" on a real basis of clandestine sensuality. In "Mrs. Warren's Profession" you had the procuress, the organiser of prostitution, convicting society of her occupation. All three plays were criticisms of a special phase, the capitalist phase, of modern organization, and their purpose was to make people thoroughly uncomfortable whilst entertaining them artistically.

But my four subsequent plays, "Arms & The Man," "Candida," "The Man of Destiny" (the one-act Napoleon piece) and the unnamed four act comedy just finished, are not "realistic" plays. They deal with life at large, with human nature as it presents itself through all economic & social phases. "Arms and The Man" is the comedy of youthful romance & disillusion, "Candida" is the poetry of the Wife & Mother—the Virgin

Mother in the true sense, & so on & so forth. Now for the funny part of it. These later plays are of course infinitely more pleasing, more charming, more popular than the earlier three. And of course the I. T. now wants one of these pleasant plays to make a popular success with, instead of sticking to its own special business & venturing on the realistic ones. It refuses to produce "The Philanderer" (written specially for it) because it is vulgar and immoral and cynically disrespectful to ladies and gentlemen; and it wants "Candida" or one of the later plays, which I of course refuse to let it have unless it is prepared to put it up in first rate style for a London run on ordinary business terms. Consequently there is no likelihood of any work by me being produced by the I. T., although "Mrs. Warren" is still talked of on both sides as eligible. You must understand however, that we are all on the friendliest terms, and that I am rather flattered than otherwise at the preference of my friends for those plays of mine which have no purpose except the purpose of all poets & dramatists as against those which are exposures of the bad side of our social system.

Excuse this long and hasty scrawl. I let you into these matters because the man who gossips best in print about them is the man who knows what is behind the gossip.

Yrs sincerely
G. Bernard Shaw.

Note Shaw's typical fair-mindedness. Obviously Golding Bright suspected the regular actor management of boycotting Shaw, who patiently explains that the reasons for his plays not being produced probably lie in the plays themselves. . . . The actor whom Shaw wanted at this date to play Marchbanks was H. V. Esmond, player and playwright; although a young man in the nineties, he specialized in elderly comedy parts, being, during Shaw's three and a half years as dramatic critic, a fairly regular member of George Alexander's company at the St. James's; although he usually appeared

in what might be called John Hare parts in the "modern" plays of
Pinero, Jones, R. C. Carton, and J. K. Jerome, he also played such
Shakespearean roles as Touchstone and Verges. Shaw objected to
his standard parts, although he always praised his acting, because
he felt that he would make an admirable juvenile—witness his desire
to have Esmond play Marchbanks. Esmond wrote plays for such
actor-managers as Alexander and the high comedian Charles Hawtrey, and occasionally acted in them himself. He married the popular actress Eva Moore, and their daughter, Jill Esmond, is well-
known on the London stage today. . . . Of Irving and *The Man of
Destiny* there will be much more written anon. . . . The play which
Daniel Frohman, the elder of the American producing brothers, was
considering was *You Never Can Tell.* Actually it first reached the
American stage under the aegis of the American Shaw-enthusiast
Arnold Daly, in a successful five months' run at the Garrick Theatre,
New York, in 1905. The London manager most interested in it was
Cyril Maude. A later note will comment on his failure to produce it.
The London Stage Society gave it a single performance in November, 1899, at the Royalty; Yorke Stephens and James Welch
were responsible for six matinées at the Strand in May, 1900;
under the Vedrenne-Barker management at the Court it was given
nine matinées in May, 1905, and a series of successful performances
in the summer of 1906. One of Shaw's most delightful light comedies, it has strangely not been much revived. . . . The reference to
Charles Wyndham and "a play not his own" is explained in a
letter from Shaw to Hesketh Pearson dated July 12, 1939. At some
unspecified time, but obviously considerably before the writing
of this letter, Wyndham had consulted Shaw about producing "an
old play by Scribe"; Shaw advised him which part to play and
suggested that Sydney Grundy translate the play rather than himself. Shaw's memory was at fault: the French play was *L'Ami des
Femmes* of Dumas *fils;* his choice of character for the actor-manager was, however, correct—De Ryons; R. C. Carton adapted the
play as *The Squire of Dames;* and Wyndham had produced it at
the Criterion on November 5, 1895. . . . The reference to "the in-
habitants of Marlboro' House" ties up with that to the "opinion of
the Prince of Wales" three sentences later. Elsewhere, writing of
Arms and the Man, I have said: "The Crown Prince, later Edward

VII, having asked who the author was and not recognizing the name, muttered quite seriously, 'Of course he's mad,' and later it was reported: 'His Royal Highness regretted that the play should have shown so disrespectful an attitude as was betrayed by the character of the chocolate-cream soldier.'" Naturally such remarks would appeal to Shaw's ironic sense of humor. . . . The reason for Shaw's linking with Ibsen's the name of the then revolutionary but now almost forgotten Hermann Sudermann was that the latter's *Heimat* (1893) had been produced the preceding June in London simultaneously by Eleanor Duse at Daly's and by Sarah Bernhardt at Drury Lane, and that scarcely a week before the date of this letter Mrs. Pat had made a sensation by appearing in a translation of the same play by Louis N. Parker, entitled *Magda*, which Shaw had reviewed at length and excitedly on June 6th. . . . The Byron referred to was not the poet, but the journalist turned successful actor-dramatist, H. J. Byron, whose farces, mainly consisting of outrageous puns, entranced the audiences of the seventies and today are not read even by specialists. His greatest hit had been *Our Boys*, which broke all existing records by running continuously from January 16, 1875, through April 18, 1879. . . . Shaw's prophecy concerning the future success of his own plays was too cautious; since his death, especially in America, his comedies have continued to score professional successes. . . . All critics of Shaw have noted the special economic bent of the very early plays. Especially interesting is a monograph by Stanley Marquis Holberg, *The Economic Rogue in the Plays of Bernard Shaw*, 1953, which studies Sartorius of *Widowers' Houses* and Mrs. Warren at considerable length. . . . Shaw's unhappy habit of referring ironically to Candida as "the Virgin Mother" has without doubt contributed a great deal in the last sixty years to encouraging the conventional misinterpretation by actresses of that exceedingly unpleasant and annoying female. . . . Again Shaw refers to Grein's cliquish producing group as "the I. T." . . . Note the early reference to himself as poet and dramatist; not long before his death November, 1950, Terence Rattigan, who should know better, ignoring the poet, launched his famed attack upon Shaw as dramatist of ideas in *The New Statesman and Nation*, but as early as 1891, in *The Quintessence of Ibsenism* (the general comments in which

Eric Bentley has rightly said may be applied to the author), Shaw had constantly insisted that the truly serious, and surely the great, dramatist was necessarily a poet in his vision of life. . . . Again Shaw emphasizes to Bright (and there is no record concerning exactly when they did meet) that he is feeding the gossip-columnist with reliable information. That it may have helped to have one journalist telling the truth about him is beside the point.

11. More Advice to a Young Journalist—and Several Practical Matters

29 Fitzroy Square W.
22nd September 1896.

Dear Bright

I have only just returned from the country for "Cymbeline." I worked hard all through the holidays, but did not succeed in answering my letters.

I enclose some press cuttings, which you may as well contradict in order to prove your omniscience to The Sun. The new play, of which I gave you the first particulars, is entitled "You Never Can Tell." Like all my plays, it contains some very tempting parts, one of which has fascinated Cyril Maude. But nothing whatever has been settled; and the announcements enclosed are altogether premature. The play is still in my hands; and you may safely conclude that it will remain there until it leaves them for production. The decision of the Haymarket management to produce a romantic play of the Zenda type seems to indicate that they have reconsidered any notion they may have had of a new departure in drama. At any rate, there is one person who will not be surprised if "You Never Can Tell" is produced elsewhere; and that person is the author.

The question of the Napoleon play at the Lyceum will be decided when "Cymbeline" is out of the way. I will let you know as soon as there is anything to publish. As the matter stands at present, Irving has made me an offer of which I have no reason to complain. But I have proposed certain conditions to which he is unaccustomed, and which he is perhaps slow to understand, though they are of no particular consequence to him; and this has hung up the affair until there is more time to consider it.

It was true enough about the bicycle accident. One afternoon in the middle of July, I was riding in Pall Mall East when a Great Western Railway van, coming out of the Haymarket, turned up Pall Mall on the wrong side owing to the horse shying at something, and charged me point blank. It was a pretty piece of tournamenting. I went ahead gallantly, and hit the horse fair and square on the breastbone with my front tyre, fully believing that the most impetuous railway van must go down before the onslaught of Bernard Shaw. But it didn't. I hit the dust like the Templar before the lance of Ivanhoe; and though I managed to roll over and spring upright with an acrobatic bound just clear of the wheels, my bike came out a mangled shrieking corpse. It was rather exciting for a sedentary literary man like myself; but I gather from your opinion of my Bayreuth articles, the following week, that I was none the worse for it internally.

Yes: the Star articles on the International Congress were by me.

I very strongly advise you to practise public speaking: it will be of great use to you. If you look in the lecture lists in the Sunday papers, or in "Justice," you will find plenty of announcements of meetings at halls and workmen's clubs about London or in the open air, where you can go and join in the discussion. I do not know what the debating societies, literary societies, and amateur local parliaments of today are—such things never last more than four years, and the ones I frequented are dead—but there must be as many of them about as ever. The Playgoers' Club is not exactly what you want; but why do you not form a genuine debating society inside it. If there are half a dozen young fellows who really want to talk out their opinions without the humbug of the big Sunday night celebrity hunting functions, they can easily agree to meet somewhere once a week, and take it in turns to get up a subject for discussion and put some work into it—not merely air their opinions and show their cleverness, but work up some information for the use of the rest. For instance, Archer once delivered a series of lectures at the Royal Institution which contained a lot of information about the modern picture stage. He might even consent to come down and talk for an hour to a little knot of fellows about it. As a rule, you will find that the better the man, the more willing he is to do a thing of that sort, and the less disposed to waste his time on windy functions like the Sunday full dress debates. However, that is by the way. Join or attend all the societies for discussion you can find, and speak every time, no matter how humiliating the result may be. Buy "The Chairman's Handbook" (or look it up in the Museum) so as to learn the technical order of public meeting. Most public men pick it up as they go along, and never to the end of their days know it properly; but it is well to be instructed in the matter, so as to be ready to take the chair if you are asked. From casual debating you might go on to delivering addresses; and be sure you don't write them out or learn them by heart: make a few notes and speak extemporaneously from them. And don't despise or funk the street corner: it is an indispensable part of a speaker's education.

You ought to join the political associations of your district, Liberal or Conservative, according to your opinions; but you had much better begin as a Socialist and have a good generous revolutionary time before settling down. Call at the Fabian office, 276 Strand, and tell Pease, the secretary, that you want to be advised how to begin. And bring a shilling to buy tracts with. If we are too slow for you, try the S.D.F. and serve a year or two under the red flag. You will make a blazing fool of yourself; but you won't regret it.

G. B. S.

For B. Shaw

DURRANT'S PRESS CUTTINGS

Established 1880.   Chief London Offices:—

57, HOLBORN VIADUCT, LONDON, E.C.

- -

Advertisements and News received for all papers.

THE ST. JAMES GAZETTE,
Dorset Street, Whitefriars, London, E.C.
(E. Southcott, Publisher)

Cutting from issue dated Sept 18 1896

"Rehearsals of 'Under the Red Robe' are proceeding vigorously, and it is expected that the Haymarket will soon reopen with that piece on October 15. We have already mentioned the principal characters of the cast, which is now completed by the engagement of Mr. J. L. Mackay (who, by the way, may be expected to blossom out as an author shortly) for the part of the Duc de Pombar, and Mr. Bernard Gould for that of the Lieutenant; while Mr. Holman Clark is to appear as Clon, the dumb man. Among other pieces secured by Messrs. Harrison and Maude are 'Leoni,' a four-act drama by Mr. H. V. Esmond, and an entirely new play by Mr. George Bernard Shaw."

Close on Saturdays at 2 o'clock.

For B. Shaw

DURRANT'S PRESS CUTTINGS

Established 1880.   Chief London Offices:—

57, HOLBORN VIADUCT, LONDON, E.C.

- -

Advertisements and News received for all papers.

THE WESTMINSTER GAZETTE.
Tudor Street, Whitefriars, London E.C.
(Printed and Published by John Marshall.)

Cutting from issue dated Sept 19 1896   ·

"The new management of the Haymarket will start well provided with plays. In addition to 'Under the Red Robe,' with which the season will open, Messrs. Frederick Harrison and Cyril Maude have secured a new play called 'Leoni,' by Mr. H. V. Esmond, which will follow the piece founded by Mr. Edward Rose upon Mr. Stanley J. Weyman's novel. They have also accepted, for production later, a play by Mr. George Bernard Shaw, whose most diverting comedy, 'Arms and the Man,' will be gratefully remembered."

Close on Saturdays at 2 o'clock.

For B. Shaw

DURRANT'S PRESS CUTTINGS

Established 1880.   Chief London Office:—

57, HOLBORN STREET, LONDON, E.C.

- -

Advertisements and News received for all papers.

___

THE LIVERPOOL DAILY COURIER,
Victoria Street, Liverpool.
(C. Tinling & Co. Publishers)

Cutting from issue dated Sept 21 1896

"Rehearsals of 'Under the Red Robe' are proceeding vigorously, and it is expected that the Haymarket will reopen with the piece on Oct. 15. The cast is now completed by the engagement of Mr. J. L. Mackay (who, by the way, may be expected to blossom out as an author shortly), for the part of the Duc de Pombar, and Mr. Bernard Gould for that of the Lieutenant, while Mr. Holman Clark will appear as Clon, the dumb man. Among other pieces secured by Messrs. Harrison and Maude are 'Leoni,' a four-act drama by Mr. H. V. Esmond, and an entirely new play by Mr. George Bernard Shaw."

Close on Saturdays at 2 o'clock.

Henry Irving produced *Cymbeline* at the Lyceum the night of the day this letter was written. Shaw's review, dated September 26th, is one of his finest and most thorough pieces of dramatic criticism. From the beginning of the month, first from London and then from the country (Stratford St. Andrew) he had been coaching Ellen Terry in the playing of Imogen; the series of letter between

critic and actress from one of the most exciting and valuable parts
of the famous Shaw-Terry *Correspondence* (pp. 30-66).

Bright, of course, was not responsible for the material in the
press cuttings. . . . There will be more mention of Cyril Maude
and *You Never Can Tell.* The "romantic play of the Zenda type"
was *Under the Red Robe,* referred to in Bright's paragraphs. It
was adapted from the popular novel of Stanley Weyman by
Edward Rose, and produced by Maude at the Haymarket on October 17th; Shaw reviewed it a week later. Shaw had his chance
to be "not surprised" at his play not following the Weyman-Rose
melodrama. The details of the first productions of *You Never Can
Tell* have been given earlier. . . . Shaw's and Ellen Terry's letters
during this time, even those concerned intensely and in detail with
Cymbeline, are filled with references to the possibility of Irving's
really producing *The Man of Destiny,* written, despite Shaw's
many later denials, for Irving and Terry. . . . Shaw had taken up
bicycling while staying with the Webbs at Beachy Head in 1895;
his typical enthusiasm for machines soon made him a devoted
cyclist, despite frequent tumbles and accidents. . . . To my knowledge the "Bayreuth articles" referred to have never been republished and I cannot find where they originally appeared. However,
Shaw summed up his opinions on Bayreuth in the final section of
The Perfect Wagnerite (1898). Neither am I familiar with "the
Star articles on the International Congress" (Shaw attended two,
one in Zurich, one in London; Henderson mentions the *Star* articles, but gives no dates), but in July Shaw had reported, in Fabian
Tract #70, on "Fabian Policy and Resolutions presented by the
Fabian Society to the International Socialist Workers and Trade
Union Congress 1896," and in this same month of September he
contributed "Socialism at the International Congress" to Sir
Winston Churchill's mother's short-lived but *de luxe* separately-
bound-in-each-issue periodical *Cosmopolis.* . . . Shaw had previously urged Bright to take up public speaking; but here he really
lets himself ride one of his pet hobbies, although again are evident
the care and the detail constant in his advice to Bright. William
Archer's lectures at the Royal Institution were, I am positive,
never published, and his brother does not even mention them in
his biography. . . . Edward R. Pease, who continued a long time

as party secretary, wrote *The History of the Fabian Society* (1916), which contains much reference to Shaw and a ten-page "Appendix and Memoranda" by him. "S. D. F." refers to the Social Democratic Federation, originally called the Democratic Foundation, founded by Henry Mayers Hyndman, which Shaw had joined in the early eighties and in which he had remained active until in May of 1884 he became interested in the more moderate Fabian Society, then meeting at the home of Pease. Note Shaw's early reference to "the red flag." . . . The play by H. V. Esmond mentioned in Bright's paragraphs seems not to have been produced. His next London play was *One Summer's Day*, produced by Charles Hawtrey at the Comedy, October 11, 1897. Neither play nor playwright is mentioned by Cyril Maude in his memoirs of his joint-management of the Haymarket.

12. A Postcard Briefing on the Status of *The Man of Destiny* and *You Never Can Tell*

29 Fitzroy Square W.
25th September 1896.

I have unluckily no news this week, as all appointments are put off until next, except one with Irving tomorrow. But as it seems that both he & the Haymarket people wish to hold on to the plays, and I cannot very well make difficulties if they are in earnest (which they now seem to be), you had better modify anything you may wish to say in the sense that the announcements in the St. James's &c were premature insofar as nothing has been finally settled, but that it is likely that the news will be true by the time it is confirmed by the omniscient Sun. Say nothing about the Lyceum until the affair is quite settled.

G. B. S.

POST CARD dated 25th Sep. 1896.

R. Golding Bright, Esq.
18 Alfred Place,
Gower Street,
W.C.

The "announcements in the St. James's &c" refers to the clippings sent with Shaw's previous letter.

13. Vagueness concerning Irving and Brief Golden Advice

29 Fitzroy Square W.
26th Sept. 1896.

Dear Bright

I enclose the news. If you don't get it into tomorrow's Sun, you will be late, as Irving will give it to Bendall on his own account.

I have hastily thrown it into paragraph form; so that if it comes in the rush of going to press you can send it to the printers without delaying to recast it.

I believe there was an Irving interview in the Chronicle (which I did not see) in which he referred to this play without naming me or it. He said, I understand, that I offered it to him; but as a matter of fact I didn't, as I consider myself barred from that by my position as critic except in the case of managers who have taken the initiative by inviting me to show them my plays. I don't want that said, but then I don't want the other things said either; so if you can burke any statement about my offering plays uninvited, do so. It was Ellen Terry who managed the affair.

Observe that I have just declared that Irving has no literary judgment (see the Saturday Review). And on the same morning he accepts a play by me! A neat dilemma—either my criticism is wrong or my play is bad.

Yes: bicycling's a capital thing for the literary man. I am delighted to hear of your holidays abroad instead of that cursed city office—I was once in an office myself. Also that you are now on your journalistic feet, and able to oblige me materially in letting my news out.

Let me give you a piece of advice. When a Shakespeare play is coming out—or a Sheridan one, or any old published one— buy a copy & stage manage it yourself, marking all the business. Then go and see it, and you will be astonished at the grip you will have of it & how much you will learn about the stage from your mistakes & theirs.

Yrs ever
G. Bernard Shaw.

Unfortunately the Bright collection of letters does not include the news enclosed. Obviously it concerned the meeting of Shaw with Irving. Bendall, one assumes, was an editor or a columnist on a rival newspaper to the *Sun*. . . . I am not familiar with the Irving interview in the *Chronicle*, and the whole matter of the Irving-Shaw incident over *The Man of Destiny* is hastily glossed over by Laurence Irving in his monumental 1951 biography of his grandfather, *Henry Irving, The Actor and His World*. On September 23 Shaw had written Irving, saying that he assumed the latter's plans to produce Sardou's *Madame Saint-Gêne*, playing Napoleon therein, implied that he had lost interest in Shaw's one-acter. Irving set an interview for September 26th, the date of this note, which obviously must have been written before Shaw met the actor-manager. Laurence Irving laments that what actually happened at the meeting, "probably one of the strangest in theatrical history," is unknown. Ellen Terry intended to join the two men, got as far as the door of Irving's office, and lost her courage. Years later Shaw wrote to Irving's son Laurence, the biographer's uncle, that he had not deliberately "demagnetized" Irving and "made him uncomfortable." Accompanying item #18, under date of May 13, 1897, below, will be found Shaw's own account, written in the third person, of the whole story of his Napoleon's fate at the Lyceum. However slanted it may have been, it is the fullest account of this famous *contretemps* yet published on the evidence of one of the participants. . . . Shaw's denial to Irving of "literary judgment" had been published in the *Cymbeline* review as a "curious want of connoisseurship in literature." . . . One wonders whether the excellent bit of advice in the closing paragraph was occasioned by a lost review by Bright of *Cymbeline,* or merely by Shaw's own recent experience of stage-managing that play in the course of his correspondence coaching of Ellen Terry. A comparison of the Terry letters with the *Saturday* review forms the perfect illustration of the trenchancy of the advice here given. I made this comparison at some length in an article published in *The Theatre Annual* for 1950.

14. Elizabeth Robins and Plans for Ibsen

29 Fitzroy Square W.
23rd October 1896.

Dear Bright

The paragraphs last week were gorgeous, especially a slip at the end, which must have thrown all London for a radius of a mile round Mrs. P. C. into convulsions. You said she was to play Winifred Emery's M O T H E R—Great Heavens, man: it's her sister.

The news now is that Ibsen is to the fore again. His new play is expected over in a few weeks; and this has so waked his disciples up to the scandal of "Little Eyolf" being still unperformed, that Miss Elizabeth Robins has flung herself into the business with all her energy; and it may now be taken as settled that "Little E" will be produced before the end of November, at a series of subscription performances, with Miss Robins as Asta and Miss Janet Achurch as Rita, that is to say, with the strongest Ibsen cast yet seen in London. Echegaray is also to have a turn. I—G.B.S., moi qui vous parle—devoted nearly a whole article to Echegaray's "Mariana" when it was published here, and pointed out that it ought to be snapped up as a star part by some enterprising emulator of Bernhardt and Duse. Miss Robins has taken the hint, and promises "Mariana" after "Little Eyolf." She has also declared, in a signed circular, that if the performances produce any profit, she will use it as the nucleus of a fund for the performance of plays which are too good to be commercially practicable. This means, in plain English, that she does not believe in the Independent Theatre, and is going to set about its work as if it did not exist. In the face of its prolonged inaction we can only say "Serve it right"; but what do Mr. Grein, and Mr. Charles Charrington, and Miss Dorothy Leighton say?

Of course this is nothing new for Miss Robins, to whose enterprise & devotion we already owe our acquaintance with "Hedda Gabler," "Karin," and "The Master Builder."

Yrs
G. B. S.

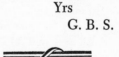

Bright's boner of the preceding week concerning Winifred Emery and Mrs. Pat is completely inexplicable to me. On October 17th, *Under the Red Robe* had opened at the Haymarket Theatre, its feminine star Winifred Emery, the wife of the actor-manager Cyril

Maude. Mrs. Pat was "at liberty" and was to appear the next month as the Ratwife in Ibsen's *Little Eyolf* with Elizabeth Robins. The only deduction I can make is that, for some unknown reason, Bright must again have been speculating upon Maude's producing *You Never Can Tell* and had suggested that Mrs. Pat was to appear in that as Mrs. Clandon. But this theory necessitates our accepting Shaw as saying that Mrs. Pat was being considered for the older daughter Gloria. Nowhere has it been suggested heretofore that this was true, nor did Mrs. Pat ever act with the Haymarket. Nowhere in Shaw biography, nowhere in Mrs. Pat's autobiography, nowhere in the G. B. S. and Mrs. Pat correspondence is there any hint of her being considered for Gloria. To anyone who knows either actress or play, the very idea is frankly inconceivable. The only fact that seems clear is that early in September, the preceding month, Winifred Emery had refused to consider Gloria and insisted upon playing the lesser part of Dolly, the feminine half of the twins, a *much* lesser part. But the play was not put into rehearsal until April of the following year and was then abandoned. The fairly voluminous records of this fiasco never mention Mrs. Pat. Aside from the obvious humor, then, of the first paragraph, its point must remain a mystery.

"Ibsen to the fore again" seems to have stuck in Shaw's mind, for his *Saturday Review* article of November 7 was to be titled "Ibsen Ahead!" . . . "His new play" was *John Gabriel Borkman*, which, as translated by Archer, Shaw was to review twice in the following January, as "Ibsen's New Play" for *The Academy* on the 16th, and as "The New Ibsen Play" in his regular *Saturday* column on the 30th. . . . Elizabeth Robins did produce *Little Eyolf* "before the end of November," on the 23rd, to be exact. She was an American actress of some means, who was fascinated by Ibsen's women, and who, encouraged by such audience-Ibsenites as Henry James, had already played Hedda Gabler and Hilda Wangel with distinction, "between spells of Adelphi melodrama," as Grein's wife, Michael Orme, wrote in his biography. As early as April 27, 1895, Shaw had reviewed the translation by James Graham of two plays by José Echegaray, *Mariana* and *The Son of Don Juan*; he had dubbed the Spanish dramatist a writer of picturesque trage-dies, "of the school of Schiller, Victor Hugo, and Verdi"; and he had specifically recommended the part of Mariana to the attention of Mrs. Pat Campbell. But although Mrs. Pat played with Elizabeth Robins first as the Ratwife and then as Rita in *Little Eyolf*, it was the American actress herself who played the lead in the Spanish play, when she produced it in a series of matinées beginning late in February, 1897. . . . According to his wife, Grein had actually resigned as an active director for the Independent Theatre in the spring of 1895, the work of direction thereafter being taken over by Dorothy Leighton (Mrs. G. C. Ashton Johnson) and the husband-and-wife team of Charles Charrington and Janet Achurch. But Charrington was known as much as director as actor, while his wife was interested only in acting. . . . In association with Marion Lea, another well-to-do American semi-professional actress, who was to marry the American playwright Langdon Mitchell, Elizabeth Robins had produced *Hedda Gabler* in the spring of 1891 and Mrs. Hugh Bell's translation of the Swedish playwright Alfhild Agrell's *Karen* (Shaw misspelled the title), and with Herbert Waring she had produced *The Master Builder* at a series of matinées beginning February 20, 1893.

15. On "Gallery Rowdyism" and a Private Joke

---

29 Fitzroy Square W.
9th March 1897.

Dear Bright

    It seems to me that the facts—leaving the morals of the thing out of the question—shew that all attempts to meet demonstrations with counter demonstrations only make matters worse, and that the right policy is to try to educate pit and gallery into dead silence and a prompt exit on the fall of the curtain (if not before) except when they feel pleased enough to clap a bit.

Here is a passage from a letter just received, signed E.H.S.

"I hope you are not, my dear G.B.S., still smarting under the recollection of the first night of 'Arms & The Man,' when a galleryite raised his voice in protest against your making an ass of yourself by addressing the audience after the play. Do not imagine that *I* was the culprit, &c &c &c &c."

In haste, yrs sincerely
G. Bernard Shaw.

The assumption from the first paragraph is that Bright had wanted to take some action in the form of "counter demonstrations" as the result of reading Shaw's March 6th column, headed "Gallery Rowdyism," ostensibly a review of J. K. Jerome's and Eden Phillpotts' *The Mac Haggis* at the Globe, opening February 25th; but over two-thirds of the remarks formed a serious and sober and scathing attack upon the behavior of the "gallery gods" who for some years had been, especially on first nights, behaving, Shaw declared, like a bestial rabble, disturbing those in the stalls and gallery and frequently terrifying players and playwrights by the animal bawling and booing which greeted them when they took calls. Shaw's obvious and deep-seated anger boiling-over had obviously drawn a sympathetic youthful response from Golding Bright and from "E. H. S." a spoofing one. I can hazard only a guess as to the identity of the second writer, but I think it is a good one. I assume that Shaw misread the middle initial, or copied it wrong in this letter, and conclude that the "letter just received" was from Edward Fordham Spence, critic for *The Westminster Gazette*, who signed his column "E. F. S.," and who in 1910 published a volume, of no particular importance, called *Our Stage and Its Critics*, in which he took at least one rather silly sideswipe at Shaw. The point of the quoted passage is clear to us—Shaw knew that Bright himself was the misbehaving galleryite of the night of April 21, 1894, and he was therefore sharing with his correspondent-disciple the reversed joke on the initialed vulgarian who was hoping to annoy him by taunting his probable ignorance of the identity of the heckler of three years past.

16. More Material for the Gossip Column

LETTER CARD

Post Mark
Mr. 10. '97.

R. Golding Bright, Esq,
"The Sun,"
Tudor St.,
E.C.

"You Never Can Tell"

—Cast—

Valentine—a dentist (Comedian—Wyndham style of part)
Allan Aynesworth.

Crampton—old man—strong part—the father Brandon Thomas.

The Waiter at the Marine Hotel—one of my finest creations
Cyril Maude.

McComas—solicitor to Crampton & Mrs. Clandon [Jack] Barnes
(Clandon is a nom-de-plume: Mrs. Clandon is Crampton's
wife)

Bohun—an eminent Q.C. (only appears in last act, but very
good character part)   [Henry] Kemble.

Mrs. Lanfrey Clandon—Crampton's wife.   Fanny Coleman.

(Gloria—her elder daughter—the heroine   Winifred Emery.

Crampton's { Dolly Clandon }   Eva Moore
children   {   } very sparkling {
           { Phil Clandon }   twins   { J. L. Mackay

There is no plot. Mrs. Clandon is a woman of advanced
opinions who has separated from her husband, a crusty old

fashioned man, and brought her children to Madeira, where they have lived for 18 years. On her return to England with the children, now grown up, they meet the father, to whose antiquated notions their modern ideas & advanced training are quite foreign. The play grows out of this incident. The four acts all take place on the same day. Place, the seaside (not further specified). Act I, in Valentine's operating room. Act II —Lunch on the terrace of the Marine Hotel. Act III—In the Hotel—afternoon. Act IV—In the hotel—evening.

P.S. My new play "The Devil's Disciple" has been copyrighted this week for production in America by Richard Mansfield.

Cyril Maude had at last decided to produce *You Never Can Tell*. As the next letter shows, *Under the Red Robe* was still playing at the Haymarket, but plans had been agreed upon, and on April 9 rehearsals actually began, with Shaw, as was his constant desire and custom when possible, reading the play to the company. With understandable excitement and enthusiasm he was here briefing his favorite columnist on the casting, on the general character types, and on plot, setting, etc. . . . "One of my finest creations" was the famous William, revealed in the last act as the father of the lawyer Bohun, called in to settle the problems of the Clandon family. He was played in 1899 and 1900 by James Welch, and in the various Court productions from 1905 through 1907 by Louis Calvert, one of Shaw's pet actors, who drove the playwright crazy but for whom he wrote many of his "finest creations," including Broadbent and Undershaft. . . . With reference to the postscript, *The Devil's Disciple*, here first mentioned in this correspondence, had been begun early in 1896 when William Terriss, ex-leading man with Irving at the Lyceum but for some years a popular matinée idol at the Adelphi under his own management, had commissioned Shaw to write him a melodrama with a plot devised by himself which to Shaw sounded like "all the plots of the melodramas he had ever played." Shaw finally wrote *The Devil's Disciple* between September and November, but when he read the play to Terriss, the actor-manager nearly fell asleep, and he took no action until Mansfield, who had already scored a hit in America in *Arms and the Man*, had actually produced it there in October, 1897. Terriss then became really interested in the play, and made an appointment to talk business with Shaw, but before the time for the meeting he was stabbed outside the stage-door of his own theatre by a madman in December, 1897. Shaw's column dated Christmas Day closed with two really moving paragraphs of tribute to the man who as actor had not understood him as critic or playwright and at whose expense he as critic had frequently waxed most merry. . . . A fairly unimportant bit of information from that scrap-bag of stray bits which is the editor's mind: at the copyright performance of this play at the Bijou, Bayswater, on April 17, 1897, Shaw himself read the part of the second lead, the Rev. Anthony Anderson, being listed on the program as "Cashel Byron," the name of the pugilist hero of his best known and most successful novel.

17. A Veritable Feast of Gossip

Private.

Lotus. Tower Hill. Dorking.
7th May, 1897.

Dear Bright

I had better let you into all the mysteries of my plays. The fact is, nothing of mine is going to be produced at all. "The Red Robe" will probably be run through the season at the Haymarket; and the public will be left to infer that it will be followed in the autumn by "You Never Can Tell." But the truth is that two of the leading parts proved too much for the resources of the Haymarket. The lady could not possibly have got through without strong support from the gentleman; and the gentleman (your friend the dentist) was hopelessly beaten by his part, which would have required Wyndham or John Drew at least to handle it. So I went to Harrison and put it to him that we had better drop the business quietly. He was very loath to admit that such a breakdown could be possible, especially as the scenery was in hand and nine tenths of the play shaping very cheerfully. But at last he recognised that the other tenth was out of the question. So we gave it up as a bad job; and now "You Never Can Tell" is not likely to be seen until it is published. But I have settled with Harrison that this story is not to be published, as it would be very hard both on the actor who was cast for a part that was (as I foretold) quite beyond him, and on the others who could have done very well. We have simply said (truly) that the Red Robe has looked up again, and that the rehearsals of "You Never Can Tell" have been discontinued for the present. I let you into the secret so that you may know what you are about in the matter and not commit yourself to announcements that won't come off. But whilst you rearrange the background of your mind, don't let the public see anything.

Another collapse is over the Lyceum play. Irving declares that my article on "Richard III" meant that he was drunk, though of course the reasons he gives for publication are those in the enclosed press cutting. The statement that he has paid me a compliment & made me a present is, under the circumstances, enough to make a saint swear. In a few days, failing any friendly arrangement with Irving, I shall tell the whole story, probably in an interview in the Daily Mail; and a very amusing story it will be. I shall have to do the interview myself, I expect; but if you care to tell Springfield that you believe you can get an interview out of me on the subject I shall bear you out unless Irving changes his attitude.

I enclose another sheet or two, containing as much as I want mentioned just now.

> In haste,
> yrs. ever
> G. Bernard Shaw.

For G. B. Shaw

DURRANT'S PRESS CUTTINGS.

Established 1880.   Chief London Office:—

57, HOLBORN STREET, LONDON, E.C.
- -

Cutting from Glasgow Herald

Dated May 4 1897

DRAMATIC AND MUSICAL

"Sir Henry Irving has, I hear, relinquished his intention of playing Napoleon Bonaparte in Mr. George Bernard Shaw's one-act play A Man of Destiny. Sir Henry Irving had provisionally accepted the piece, but he now finds the character unsuited to him, and, moreover, as there is little chance of producing any half-programme work at the Lyceum for many months to come, he has thought it best to return the manuscript to the author with, it is understood, a handsome compliment and a present. The story of Mr. Shaw's sketch is, it may be recollected, that of an incident in the first Italian campaign, when Bonaparte and other Republican officers endeavoured to secure some compromising letters from a seductive lady who was staying at a roadside inn. The part of the lady conspirator was to have been played by Miss Ellen Terry. It may now not impossibly go to the Haymarket."

Close on Saturday at 2 o'clock.

—Things you may mention—Work it up as <u>news</u> in your own way, not as communicated by me to the paper in the first person—you will know how to manage it.

1. I have been elected a member of the St. Pancras Vestry. At the first general election of Vestries under the Local Government Act of 1894 it was urged that public spirited men of some standing should come forward & offer to serve. I condescended to do this and was ignominiously defeated, my sympathy with

Labor being considered disreputable by the workmen of St. Pancras. Now the Conservatives and Unionists and Moderates and other respectables of the parish have returned me unopposed in spite of my vehement protests that I have no time for such work. I recognise, however, that there is better work to be done in the Vestry than in the theatre, and have submitted to take my turn.

2. I have resolved to accept an offer made me by Mr. Grant Richards for the publication of my plays. I am not a disappointed dramatist, as the curiosity and interest in my plays by managers, and their friendliness and accessibility for me, have exceeded anything I had any right to expect. But in the present condition of the theatre it is evident that a dramatist like Ibsen, who absolutely disregards the conditions which managers are subject to, and throws himself on the reading public, is taking the only course in which any serious advance is possible, especially if his dramas demand much technical skill from the actors. So I have made up my mind to put my plays into print and trouble the theatre no further with them. The present proposal is to issue two volumes entitled "Plays, Pleasant and Unpleasant." Vol. I, "Unpleasant" will contain "The Philanderer" and the appalling "Mrs. Warren's Profession" with perhaps a reprint of "Widowers' Houses." Vol. II, "Pleasant," will contain "Arms and The Man," "Candida," and "You Never Can Tell." Possibly also "The Devil's Disciple" and "The Man of Destiny."

I decline to say anything more at present about Sir Henry Irving and "The Man of Destiny" except that the story, when I tell it—and I shall probably tell it very soon—will be quite as amusing as a Lyceum performance of the play would have been. None of the paragraphs in circulation convey the remotest approximation of the truth; and the statement that Sir Henry returned the MS "with a handsome compliment and a present" is a particularly audacious invention. This is enough for one week, I think.

The cheerful ironic anticlimax of the second sentence following so fast upon the first is a good example of one of the lighter forms of Shavian humor. . . . Aside from the failure of Allan Aynesworth as Valentine and of Winifred Emery as Gloria (she had been lured back to that part by Shaw at the reading-rehearsal of April 9 noted above), there had been from the beginning serious troubles. Fanny Coleman and Jack Barnes, upon hearing Shaw read the play, had immediately thrown up their parts. Kate Bishop and Sydney Valentine replaced them, but aside from Maude himself and Brandon Thomas, the rest of the cast, trained in a flamboyant style of melodramatic or what Shaw himself might have called "Pinerotic" acting, were entirely baffled by the lightness of Shaw's wit and the easy style of playing demanded by the characters, and the rehearsals, attended and largely directed by the dramatist, degenerated into a war of attrition between players and author and finally into sheer shambles. So, as Shaw writes, he and Maude's partner, the non-acting manager Frederic Harrison, agreed to call the whole thing off. . . . Incidentally, although Shaw here asks for Charles Wyndham or Augustin Daly's leading man, the popular American matinée idol John Drew, uncle of the three Barrymores, to play Valentine, he actually had hoped Maude, who, like the aforementioned H. V. Esmond, had a passion for playing old men's parts, would play the young dentist. When finally Maude, in November of this year, appeared in the title role of James M. Barrie's own dramatization of his novel, *The Little Minister*, he was probably surprised at the tremendous success he scored by finally taking Shaw's advice and exploiting what Shaw termed his "remarkable charm of quaintly naive youthfulness." . . . Although in May, 1897, Harrison and Shaw had agreed to keep the story of the rehearsals a secret, when Maude in 1903 wrote his first volume of reminiscences, *The Haymarket Theatre*, chapter XVI, written by Shaw himself in the third person and spoofing himself most of all, gave a full and hilarious account of what seven years earlier must have been a nerve-wracking and frustrating experience for all concerned.

Since Irving's *Richard III* had been produced on December 19, 1896, and Shaw's review, "Richard Himself Again," had appeared a week later, it seems a bit peculiar that the actor should wait for over four months to avenge himself for what he and his friends regarded as an insult. As a matter of fact, except for some criticism of Irving for miscasting Lena Ashwell as Prince Edward, and Gordon Craig, Ellen Terry's son, as Edward IV, Shaw's review was not devastating. But in one paragraph, devoted to mention of mis-readings, audible comments to supporting players, and some either inadequate or overdone action, Shaw did begin by saying that in "the heavy single-handed scenes" Irving seemed not to be "answering his helm satisfactorily," and ended by suggesting that the final combat looked like an attempt to imitate Edmund Kean's death scene described by Hazlitt and commenting that audiences of the nineties would probably find Kean's exaggerated acting "as absurd as his habit of lying down on a sofa when he was too tired or too drunk to keep his feet during the final scenes." In 1939, writing to Hesketh Pearson, Shaw called his notice "faithful but extremely stupid . . . stupid because I ought to have seen that what was the matter was that he had drunk a little too much," an idea which he denied having had while viewing the first night or writing the review. But Irving and his lieutenants took the paragraph as a public accusation of drunkenness, and poor Shaw was attacked on all sides, except that he understood that the actor's son H. B. commented that "it served the old man right and would teach him to keep sober the next time." (There was little love lost at any time between Irving and his sons.) . . . Those who prefer to hear the actor-manager's defense should read pp. 594-607 of H. B.'s son's idolatrous biography of H. B.'s father. He accepts, for instance, Irving's claim in a letter to Shaw, probably written just before or around the date of this letter to Bright, that he had not read the *Richard* criticism or any other criticism of Shaw's. This might be true, but it is incredible that his yes-men like L. F. Austin and Bram Stoker or his many admirers from the audience should let him remain ignorant of such a paragraph as Shaw, following the principles of critical integrity he had preached for so long to Bright, and describing what he actually saw and heard, had written in all good faith. . . . Springfield, we discover in Shaw's next letter, was the editor of *The Daily Mail.* It was a typically generous offer to suggest to Bright, a staff-member of *The Sun,* that he free-lance the interview (given to him already prepared by Shaw) to a rival paper. . . . Following the clipping that Shaw refers to come the notes mentioned in the last sentence. . . . Notice that Shaw wants Bright to revise these as he wishes; Shaw did not always, that is, dictate his own interviews. Important as a personal interview with Shaw might have been to Bright, the older critic and journalist perceives the importance of a young journalist's apparent ability to dig up news for himself. Dishonest? Definitely no. Shaw had been helped by friends, very especially by William Archer, in his own journalistic apprenticeship, and, aside from his inherent and constant generosity, he may well have been trying in turn to give such aid as he could to beginners. . . . We have noted Shaw's work as Vestryman and Borough Councillor; the public-spiritedness shown in the first note made him continue in this work, despite constantly increasing and demanding personal work and business, until 1903 before he resigned from the St. Pancras Borough Council. . . . The arrangement between Shaw and Grant Richards seems to have been a very pleasant one. *Plays Pleasant and Unpleasant* duly appeared in 1898; *The Man of Destiny* was included in the second volume, *The Pleasant Plays*; *The Devil's Disciple* appeared with *Caesar and Cleopatra* and *Captain Brassbound's Conversion*, also published by Richards, in 1901 in a volume titled *Three Plays for Puritans.* . . . The point of the "reprint" of *Widowers' Houses* is that the Independent Theatre had sponsored a publication of it after they had first produced it.

18. Shaw Interviews Himself on *The Man of Destiny* Muddle

29 Fitzroy Square W.
13th May 1897.

Dear Bright

You will understand that dirty linen must not be washed in public, and that the most fatal character to appear before the public in is that of a man with a grievance. So I must walk out of the Lyceum arm in arm with Irving.

I enclose you the conversational part of an interview, which you can fit with any introduction you please. I send with it one of the counterparts of the agreement alluded to in the interview; so that you may have the evidence in your hand. Please return it.

The Daily Mail is, I think, the best mark for the interview, as Springfield invited me to speak myself on the subject in it. The Star also sent a man to me; and the editor, Ernest Parke, is very friendly to me. I greatly regret that I am a day too late to have a copy of the interview in the hands of Clement Scott before he writes his Saturday column (I wonder would the D. M. give an advance proof for him) and of the other Saturday men. However, it doesn't greatly matter. Make them put it in Saturday's paper at all events.

> In haste, yrs sincerely
> G. Bernard Shaw.

During the last fortnight or so, no man has been so liberally be-paragraphed in the Dramatic World as Mr. Bernard Shaw, none more consistently abused on the one side, more assiduously lauded on the other—and according as the taste of the writer ran anti-Ibsen-wards or the reverse. Just as the announcement, some eighteen months ago, that Sir Henry Irving had accepted a one-act play entitled "The Man of Destiny" from "The Saturday Review" set the town by the ears in amazement that this most modern of the moderns, high priest to Ibsen and contemner of Shakespeare, had gained admission to the shrine of the Lyceum, sacred to the memory of "W. S."; so the statement, which has been current within the past few weeks to the effect that the play is now once again in the author's hands, has been the signal for many a tongue to start clattering. Wherever two or three were gathered together, there the subject of "G. B. S." and "A Man of Destiny" cropped up and, so surely, one of the party would assume an air of mystery

—wholly foreign to his nature—and with some doubtful phrase as "I could an I would" or "were I not in honour bound," assert that he individually had some inner knowledge of the affair denied to the meaner herd. This state of things was obviously destined to end and, judging from the absolutely opposed statements scattered broadcast, that the psychological moment for an official pronouncement had arrived, a representative of this paper set out in search of the same. As the portals of the Lyceum however, bear the Dante legend "all hope abandon, ye who enter here"—to journalists and seekers after "copy"— his feet led him past Willington Street in a westerly direction to Fitzroy Square.

Having climbed innumerable stairs, knocked at a door and been cordially welcomed on the doormat, he subsided into the nearest available chair and after a brief rest for recovery of breath et cetera, plunged in medias res with the query:—

"Can you be persuaded to say anything about the reports which have been circulating as to your Lyceum play?"

"By all means. Do you want the history from the beginning?" was the courteous reply.

"If you please, Mr. Shaw."

"Well, the matter is very simple. About eighteen months ago, when Sir Henry Irving was touring in America, one of my admirers shewed him a trumpery little one-act play of mine called "The Man of Destiny." Sir Henry, whose literary judgment is his weak point, enormously overrated the play, and made me an offer for it. I, of course, held the play at his disposal and made no further attempt to deal with it; but I put the business off until he should have time to think twice about it. Nothing more passed until the night when he announced from the stage his intention of producing "Madame Sans-Gène." I then represented to him that he could not very well play the two Napoleons—Sardou's and mine, and proposed that we should cry off. But I found him still obstinately under the spell of my genius. He saw no reason why he should not play the two—he had always wanted to play the young Napoleon—he had a medallion of him—he had looked like him in the last act of Claude Melnotte—the part gave him what was missing in the older, coarser Napoleon of forty in "Sans-Gène", in fact he gave me a thousand and one reasons for keeping to his resolution. I told him he overrated the play, and offered to write him a better one. He provoked me extremely by assuring me, with unmistakeable sincerity, that he was sure I should never write a better one: in fact, I think he was surprised that I had written anything so good. It was on this point that our main difficulty arose. Sir Henry Irving wanted to be free to produce the play when he could really do it justice by arranging for a run: I, on the other hand, declared that I had rather destroy the piece than have it produced as my latest achievement at some remote date when I had long outgrown it. In the end, he very reluctantly agreed to produce it before the end of the present year (this passed, you must understand, in July 1896 or thereabouts). A contract was drawn up: here it is!"—and with this the portentous-looking document, full of legal technicalities, duly signed and witnessed by Miss Edith Wardell (Miss Edith Craig) was placed in my hands. "If you look through the clauses you will see that it is not an ordinary commercial affair. Sir Henry desired that we should deal with one another as men of honour; and I accepted that basis gladly. You see!— there is no question of money, no advances, no penalties, a very modest fee (as such things go) for actual performances, payable out of the money paid by the public, and ample reservations to Sir Henry Irving of performing rights both here and in America, without any of the usual pecuniary considerations which attend such reservations. But, please, let it be clear that this is not due to any illiberality on Sir Henry Irving's part. He gave me practically carte blanche as to money terms; but my position as a dramatic critic ties my hands in respect of advances and penalties, and prevents managers from objecting to special arrangements, which have a great air of being nobly disinterested on my part, but which are—as a matter of fact—inconvenient and exasperating in the highest degree to the unfortunate managers. You see then, that the agreement, though it effectually locked up my play, only bound Sir Henry Irving to produce before the end of 1897; and, by providing no penalty for non-compliance, left even that on the footing of an understanding, (in Sir Henry's own phrase) between men of honour. You may take the agreement away and study it if you like; for I think it effectually disposes of the inventions which have been circulating recently as to the spirit in which Sir Henry Irving and I dealt with one another."

"But is the play to be produced, then, after all?"

"No! That is the second chapter of the story. The lapse of a year brings many dillusions with it; and I suspect that when "Madame Sans-Gène" brought Sir Henry Irving face to face with his rash engagement to play Napoleon twice, he began to realise what a piffling little affair this play of mine is, and how extremely difficult it would be to fit it into the Lyceum bill. Naturally, he has not recanted his former opinion of the play to me, whatever his private sentiments may be; but after the accident which interrupted the career of "Richard III" and upset his arrangements for the season, we had a correspondence from which I gathered that, if I insisted on my pound of flesh in the shape of a production of the play this year, I should put him in a very disagreeable situation. His desire was that I should leave him free to produce it a little later, with a view to combining it with a certain play by one of our leading dramatists, which will create a good deal of interest when it is produced at the Lyceum. But I held to my old position, and preferred to settle the difficulty by cancelling the agreement, getting the play back, and crying off the whole bargain.

"Unfortunately, secrets in London are never more than half kept; and before the conclusion of the matter left me at liberty to speak, a paragraph appeared stating that a play of mine had been rejected at the Lyceum. Immediately the cry was taken up on all hands and garnished with all sorts of ridiculous inventions. Our good old anti-Ibsenite grandmother, "The Era," solemnly scolded the wicked people who had stated that plays by wicked people like myself were accepted at the Lyceum Theatre. A London correspondent, with a clever air of inside knowledge, described how my play had been returned "with a handsome present." One stupendous ass explained that Sir Henry returned "The Man of Destiny" to rebuke me for writing excessively adulatory articles about him in the "Saturday Review." All this nonsense seems to have created an appetite for a few authoritative words on the real state of the case. Well, you have them. Are you satisfied?"

"Somewhat disappointed that we are not to see your play, Mr. Shaw."

"You need not be. My reputation as a dramatist grows with every play of mine that is *not* performed. Besides, Irving should go to the real Man of Destiny—Ibsen. 'A Doll's House,' 'Borkman,' eh?"

The rest of Mr. Shaw's conversation was not directed to the Lyceum affair.

Of the letter itself I think only two things need be said: first, despite Shaw's natural desire to have his account of the final break with Irving in all the Saturday papers, he took care to be sure that Bright got the manuscript and gave him some liberty of editing, and second, despite his personal opinion of the critic and the steady divergence in idea and method between Clement Scott and himself, still, with his unconquerable fairness, he laments seeming to have scooped his enemy on *The Daily Telegraph*.

Few points in Shaw's manuscript need elucidation. The imaginary interviewer headed for Fitzroy Square, of course, because Shaw lived there, at 29 W. . . . The "admirer" who could show Irving *The Man of Destiny* during an American tour could obviously be no other than Ellen herself. He mentioned the play to her in a letter dated November 1, 1895, and, on her urgent request, sent it to her on November 28th. She immediately began what Christopher St. John called her "campaign" to make Irving promise to produce the play. . . . The letter in which Shaw proposed "that we should cry off" is printed in Laurence Irving's biography,

p. 594. Shaw made, especially for him, a most unusual mistake in date by mentioning "July 1896 or thereabouts," for his letter to Irving, printed by the grandson, is dated September 23rd, and we know that he told Bright on the 25th that the famous interview, here for the first time in book-form described in detail by one of the participants, was to take place "tomorrow." On the same day he wrote Ellen Terry the same information, specifying that the "conference" was set for "midday," and expressing his fear that his interest, on first meeting, in Irving as a *person* would drive from his mind all thought of his "rubbishy little play" (note the probable unconscious memory when, thinking of Ellen early in the interview as "one of [his] admirers," he used the slight paraphrase, "trumpery little one-act play") . . . . Claude Melnotte was the lower-class hero of Bulwer-Lytton's sentimental romance, *The Lady of Lyons,* tremendously popular with nineteenth-century audiences but now happily forgotten. . . . Edith Ailsa Geraldine Craig was Ellen's daughter, and at the time of the Irving-Shaw meeting was playing minor parts at the Lyceum; apparently, being in the theatre, she was asked to witness the signatures on the lost contract. One wonders whether it was innate courtesy and tact (it could scarcely have been ignorance) that made Shaw refer to her by the last name of Ellen Terry's second husband, Charles Wardell; although she and her brother, Edward Gordon, were both called Craig by their mother, they were the illegitimate children of Ellen Terry and Edward Godwin. . . . The "accident which interrupted the career" of *Richard III* happened when Irving returned to his rooms after the first night. According to his grandson, "on his way up the narrow stairs he slipped and struck his knee against a chest which stood upon the landing," the result being the rupturing of the ligatures of his knee-cap, and his incapacitation for some weeks. Shaw, writing to Pearson in 1939, said that the reason why his own apparent claim that the actor was drunk that first night had caused such a stir was that he *was* drunk, and that Irving "fell downstairs." Well, who can say now? At least the Shakespeare play had to be called off until the end of February. . . . If Shaw's memory was accurate and if Irving was sincere in offering to combine *The Man of Destiny* "with a certain play by one of our leading dramatists," then the actor-manager changed his plans, for

Madame Sans-Gène was followed at the Lyceum by a work written by Irving's second son, *Peter the Great*, and the next production was *The Medicine Man*, by the scholar H. D. Traill and Shaw's successor as music critic on *The World*, Robert Hichens. None of these men was qualified to rate as "one of our leading dramatists." . . . *The Era* was a weekly newspaper devoted entirely to theatrical and sporting news. . . . Shaw was quite serious in suggesting that Irving should play Ibsen's John Gabriel Borkman, although I suspect him of an ironic dig in the reference to Torvald Helmer as suitable for the Lord of the Lyceum. In both the *Academy* and the *Saturday Review* essays on the play when it first appeared in book form, Shaw had suggested (as also had his friend and brother-critic of *The Times*, A. B. Walkley) that the three leading roles in Ibsen's play were ideally suited to Irving, Ellen Terry, and the American actress Geneviève Ward, then a member of the Lyceum company. . . . Finally, the reader interested in the full account here given by Shaw of the meeting between actor and dramatist is referred to the letter to Pearson mentioned above (in his *Full Length Portrait*, pp. 138-140, and to the Shaw-Terry correspondence ranging from November 1, 1895, on and off through May 24, 1897. Incidentally, in a letter to Ellen written on the same day that he sent the interview to Bright, Shaw told her to watch for the interview and made one of the few references to Bright that I have discovered, saying that he had used his version of the meeting "to give a chance to a young journalist in whom I am interested." Ellen, when she had read the interview, became angry, insofar as the dear creature was capable of anger, at both men, neither of whom seemed to care as she did for "THE PLAY."

19. Advice to Attend a Première

29 Fitzroy Square W.
11th June, 1897.

Dear Bright

I should not be surprised if "The Man of Destiny" were to take a trial trip at Croydon on the 28th, with Murray Carson as the one and only Napoleon. I don't know whether he has succeeded in fixing this, but I have given my consent; and I am not aware that there are any special difficulties in the way.

yrs sincerely
G. Bernard Shaw.

LETTER CARD

Post marked
Ju. 11 '97

R. Golding Bright Esq,
"The Sun"
Tudor Street,
E.C.

Shaw was wrong only as to date; Murray Carson, an actor-friend of the critic-playwright, produced *The Man of Destiny* for three performances at the Grand Theatre, Croydon, July 1, 2, and 3, 1897. . . . Granville-Barker played Napoleon for one matinée performance sponsored by Grein at the Comedy Theatre, March 29, 1901. . . . Arnold Daly added to his Shavian repertory the part of the young Napoleon during the season of 1903–1904. . . . The younger Dion Boucicault and his wife Irene Vanbrugh played it for eight matinées at the Court in June, 1907. . . . Murray Carson, incidentally, also gave the first English production of *The Devil's Disciple* at the Prince of Wales Theatre, Kennington, September 28, 1899 (thirteen performances).

20. Some Lyceum Gossip for Golding Bright

29 Fitzroy Square W.
16th July 1897.

The deadest secret of the week is, that Mr. Laurence Irving has completed a five-act play which has produced such a powerful impression in the family circle that its production in an obvious quarter (not usually a likely one for young dramatic authors) has been privately determined on. Moral: do not make your deadest secrets the main topic of conversation at the Women's Jubilee Dinner.

You may safely venture on the above, or some paraphrase of it.

G. B. S.

LETTER CARD

Post marked
Ju. 16 '97

R. Golding Bright Esq,
"The Sun"
Tudor St
E.C.

Peter the Great, written by Irving's younger son, Laurence, uncle of the biographer, was produced at the Lyceum January 1, 1898. A week later Shaw reviewed, under the heading "Peter the Blackguard," the play-script only, which he had read "some time ago" and which he analyzed in detail and praised highly as being, despite the romantic material, "essentially modern and realistic." Of the production he remarked "Heaven" and his "fellow-critics" could speak; he could not, since Irving, still carrying on the feud occasioned by Shaw's review of *Richard III*, had not given tickets to *The Saturday Review*, which omission Shaw took as "an appeal to one to stay away." . . . For all his willingness to speak anywhere at any time on any subject, I cannot conceive what Shaw was doing at the Women's Jubilee Dinner. There is no record in any of the standard biographies of his having attended. Someone, of course, may have brought him some gossip from the dinner. July, 1897, was the month of Victoria's Jubilee celebration. Shaw had referred to it a couple of weeks earlier in his July 3rd column, "Ghosts at the Jubilee," one of the most moving and powerful pieces of criticism he ever wrote, one in which he used the Independent Theatre revival of *Ghosts*, with Mrs. Theodore Wright again playing Mrs. Alving, as a thread about which to weave a criticism of the Victorian period up to 1897.

21. Advice on *Plays, Pleasant and Unpleasant*

29 Fitzroy Square W.
11th March 1898

Unfortunately, I did not get a chance of acting promptly on your letter, as I was away when it arrived. I sent all the stuff on. It is much too long from the editorial point of view; but they can select what they want. If they know their business they will drop the first half rather than the second. I have altered a few words, because the book in its present form has changed a little in its way through the press since I wrote to you. We hope to get it out by the middle of April: it is all passed for press now; and nothing delays us but the American edition, which must, of course, appear simultaneously. Thanks.

G. Bernard Shaw

POST CARD

Post marked
11th Mch 98

R. Golding Bright Esq.
2 Augusta Road
Ramsgate

"Wky. Sun"
Mch. 20, 98.

THE PLAYS OF "G. B. S."

Some account of his forthcoming volumes.

("Weekly Sun" Special.)

The polemics of Mr. Bernard Shaw—whether social, political, dramatical, or personal—are an unfailing source of delight to his readers, and even those who have writhed under the heavy lash of his wit and invective have been known to join heartily in the general laugh against themselves. A sense of expectancy, therefore, hangs around the publication by Mr. Grant Richards a month hence of the critic-dramatist's collected "Plays, Pleasant and Unpleasant," in two volumes.

The familiar gibe, that publication is the last resource of the disappointed dramatist, will not hold water in this instance, for in at least two cases negotiations with West-end managers had reached the stamped agreement and rehearsal stages, only to be broken off at the eleventh hour. Perhaps, in his prefaces to these volumes, the author has seen fit to enlighten a mystified world on the subject; but who shall prophecy? You never can tell with "G.B.S." who can be provokingly discreet when he chooses.

SHAKESPEARE'S LOST OPPORTUNITY.

That the two volumes will be replete with startling innovations and split infinitives, everyone may well imagine, but I am now enabled to offer the public a more specific foretaste of the pleasures which await them. Like Ibsen, Mr. Shaw realizes that, by disregarding the conditions under which managers labour and by throwing himself on the reading public, a dramatist is taking the only course by which any serious advance is possible. But unlike the Scandinavian, he has very decided views as to the futility of offering readers a mere reproduction of the "prompt copies" prepared for stage use. "The dramatic author must," he contends in one of these prefaces, "fall back on his powers of literary expression, as other poets and fictionists do. . . . What would we not give for the copy of Hamlet used by Shakespeare at rehearsal, with the original 'business' scrawled by the prompter's pencil? And if we had, in addition, the descriptive directions which the author gave on the stage—above all, the character sketches, however brief, by which he tried to convey to the actor the sort of person he wished him to incarnate—what a light they would shed, not only on the play, but on the history of the sixteenth century! . . . It is for the want of this process of elaboration that Shakespeare—unsurpassed as poet, story-teller, character draughtsman, humorist, and rhetorician—has left us no intellectually coherent drama, and could not pursue a genuinely scientific method in his studies of character and society."

Having thus spelt "w-i-n-d-e-r" in the most approved Squeers fashion, "G.B.S." proceeds to the cleaning in his own style. The familiar stage directions and scenic specifications have been abolished, and in their places will be finished—not to say ornate—descriptions, vivid character-sketches, psychologic notes and sallies of a characteristically mordant type.

SOCIETY THROUGH FABIAN GLASSES.

Volume I. consists of those plays which the author is pleased to term "unpleasant"—the unpleasantness lying in the fact that they convict the capitalistic phase of modern social organization, and are written from the point of view of a Socialist who regards the basis of middle-class society as thoroughly rotten, economically and morally. Under this heading come "Widowers' Houses," "The Philanderer," and "Mrs. Warren's Profession". The root idea of the first-named was the rich suburban villa standing on the rents of the foul rookery; of the second, a four-act topical comedy, the fashionable cults of Ibsenism and "New Womanism" on a basis of clandestine sensuality—the Independent Theatre refused to produce it on account of its "immorality!" whilst in the third, Mrs. Warren taxes society with her occupation.

The particular "profession" with which this lady is concerned is no less indecorous a one than prostitution. But she herself is far worse than a common prostitute; she is a procuress, who owns and manages brothels in all the big European cities and is not ashamed of her trade. Her gains go to the respectable bringing-up of her daughter in total ignorance of the source of her mother's income. The crux of the drama lies in the girl's enlightenment and the ensuing consequences, which, though cruel and bitter enough to satisfy the most hardened "moralist", are all quite reasonable and sober. There is no dodging, on the part of the author, around the handy corner of suicide; Mrs. Warren's conscience is not awakened to maudlin regrets of what she was at the age of sixteen; and, in fact, it is all as remorseless and appalling as the "Confessions" of Rousseau, or the vivisection of womanhood by Schopenhauer. In the heroine will be shown the real New Woman, a highly-educated, capable, independent girl of the governing classes; working, smoking, and unaffectedly preferring the society of men to that of women, because they talk of the things which interest her, and not of servants and babies, the ever recurring evils of married life. Her peculiar charm is that she plays the part of the charming woman only as the amusement of her life, not as its serious occupation.

Volume II—"Pleasant Plays"—will comprise "Arms and the Man," the sparkling comedy in three acts, of youthful romance and disillusion, which was the despair of the critics on its production at the Avenue in 1894; "The Man of Destiny," a one-act comedy, in which Sir Henry Irving had intended to appear as the youthful Napoleon; "You Never Can Tell," a four-act modern comedy concerned with the adventures of a sparkling pair of twins; and "Candida," a frankly sentimental play, which Mr. Shaw hopes to find understanded of women, if not of men.

IN DEFENCE OF THE MANAGERS.

It says much for his unfailing optimism that, despite the non-fulfilment of contracts, Mr. Shaw strongly combats the suggestion of that dramatic "ring" whose existence is so frequently deplored by Mr. Sydney Grundy. "There is no 'ring'," he asseverates vehemently, "there never really is. The fact is the business of a manager is too difficult and hazardous to admit of any trifling with 'rings' or the like. Twenty years ago Grundy complained fiercely that there was a 'ring', because no manager would touch his plays so long as there was one by Byron to be had, or the then inevitable adaptation from the French. Nowadays, no manager will produce a new man's play so long as there is one by Grundy available—or Jones, or Pinero, or Carton, or Louis Parker, &c. But why should an untried man be preferred to a tried one? There is no 'ring'—there never is, never has been, never will be, although there always seems to be one to the younger generation battering at the door."

R. G. B.

Bright's letter, referred to, must have prefaced the before-publication review of *Plays, Pleasant and Unpleasant*, given above. One regrets that the correspondence includes only Bright's review as published in *The Weekly Sun* nine days later, for obviously Shaw had again edited a Bright manuscript, though not so much in detail as he had the review of *Odette* in December of 1894. One judges "they" (the editors of *The Sun*) did not "drop" much, if anything. The first collection, in two volumes, of Shaw's plays appeared duly and simultaneously, in England under the Grant Richards imprint and in America under that of Herbert S. Stone and Company, of Chicago.

The review itself, as early Shaw criticism, is fairly good. There are some good-natured digs at his mentor, "provokingly discreet when he chooses." Good-natured, one trusts, for Bright could not seriously have complained that he had not received special favors as a gossip-columnist; indeed, he obviously wrote much of this review with Shaw's previous letters to him before him. There is, for instance, much direct quotation or paraphrase in the second and third paragraphs from Shaw's letter of June 10, 1896. As one who pedantically loathes the split infinitive, I cannot believe that for thirty years or more I have overlooked it as a Shavian habit. Bright had also obviously seen some at least of the proofs for the forthcoming volume, since he quoted from one of the prefaces— and chose wisely. . . . Wackford Squeers, eccentric master of Dotheboys Hall, in Dickens' *Nicholas Nickleby*, in "the first class in English spelling and philosophy," explains to Nicholas "the practical mode of teaching, Nickleby; the regular education system." His first illustration is: "C-l-e-a-n, clean, verb active, to make bright, to scour. W-i-n, win, d-e-r, der, winder, a casement. When the boy knows this out of the book, he goes and does it." If Bright's analogy was a bit far-fetched, it still had a certain cleverness. . . . The paragraph on *Mrs. Warren's Profession* is a paraphrase of the second paragraph in Shaw's letter of November 4, 1895. . . . The emphasis upon the "sparkling pair of twins" in *You Never Can Tell* shows that, if Bright had read one of the prefaces, he had certainly *not* read that play. . . . The final paragraph, while posing as a direct quotation (and the reader of *The Sun* might well have expected to find it in a preface in the forthcoming volumes), is a pastiche of Shaw's comments in the June 10, 1896, letter.

22. A Baffler

14th March 1898
29, Fitzroy Square, W.

Dear Mr. Bright

Enclosed is the result of my very feeble attempt to write to you on Friday. I meant to bring your letter to the telegraph office & copy your address from it. Unfortunately, I forgot it, and had to make a violent effort of memory, with what success you may see for yourself.

Yrs sincerely,
G. Bernard Shaw.

Since the enclosure is not included in the correspondence, this brief note will probably remain forever unintelligible and impenetrable.

23. Advice about Another Production-Fiasco

29 Fitzroy Square, W.
7th April 1898.

Dear Mr. Bright

Thanks, yes: I saw your notice. The date of publication is fixed for the 15th inst.

There is a hitch about "The Devil's Disciple." The only theatre Waring could get was the Lyric, and that only conditionally, Arthur Roberts being in possession. If the business of "Dandy Dan" can be worked up to a certain figure, Roberts can hold on for the season: if not, Waring can come in next month; but in the meantime it is impossible to make engagements & begin rehearsals. This cannot be explained definitely to the public, as of course the particulars about Roberts are confidential: all that can be said is that if the run of "Dandy Dan" closes in time for a new piece, the new piece will be "The D's D", and the actor-manager Waring. If, however, "Dandy Dan" holds out, it is not certain that I will consent to a production in October, because I have not had a day's real holiday for four years, and if I have to spend the autumn recess in town rehearsing, I shall risk a breakdown. And so all is uncertainty for the moment. The cast has been agreed upon; but until the engagements are actually offered and accepted, it cannot be announced. But if you care to hazard an entirely unauthorized guess, your best selection would be Lena Ashwell, Hilda Hanbury and Mrs. Crowe, with Waring, Macklin, Bourchier, Playfair and Foss. But remember that I have no right to assume that any of these, except perhaps Macklin & Bourchier, will accept parts or be available. You must guess on your own responsibility.   G. Bernard Shaw.

LETTER CARD

Post marked
Ap. 7, '98.

R. Golding Bright, Esq,
"The Sun"
Tudor St
E.C.

What more could Shaw say than admit that he had seen the "notice"? Since he had, wittingly or not, written most of it, he could scarcely criticize it. The publication date is, of course, for the two volumes of *Plays*. . . . Until I read these letters, I had not known that Herbert Waring, popular matinée idol of varied experience from first performances of Ibsen in England with Elizabeth Robins to membership in Alexander's St. James's and Maude's Haymarket companies, had ever considered producing *The Devil's Disciple*. None of the Shaw biographers mentions it. . . . Arthur Roberts was an extremely popular but rather vulgar low comedian star in musical farces whose appearances Shaw had frequently reviewed, usually with disdain. He did not, however, notice *Dandy Dan, the Lifeguardsman*, a musical comedy in two acts, by Basil Hood, with music by Walter Slaughter, which had opened at the Lyric, December 4, 1897. . . . Notice the reference to Shaw's "rehearsing." Whenever possible throughout his career he did rehearse his plays, either as acknowledged director or as invaluable "man behind" the producer. . . . Of the cast members mentioned, aside from Waring, Lena Ashwell was an established leading lady fast growing in popularity who was eventually to create the part of Lina Szczipanowska in Shaw's *Misalliance* in 1910; F. H. Macklin was a character-actor of much experience who was to play the Rev. Anthony Anderson to Murray Carson's Dick Dudgeon in the first English production late the following year; Arthur Bourchier was another popular actor of considerable talent and experience, the husband of Violet Vanbrugh, probably being considered for Burgoyne; Arthur Playfair, a comedian, was a cousin of the actor-manager Nigel, later famous as the producer of many famous revivals at the Lyric Theatre, Hammersmith. George R. Foss had been Shaw's stage manager when he directed *Arms and the Man* for Florence Farr. He was to attain considerable reputation as a Shakespearean director and write (in 1932) a fine book on producing Shakespeare, much unappreciated, *What the Author Meant*. . . . Had Waring's project worked out, it would have had a strong cast and with Shaw directing would undoubtedly have been a splendid production. After Carson's production in 1899, *The Devil's Disciple* did not reach metropolitan London until 1907, when Matheson Lang played Dick Dudgeon for the Court production. Forbes Robertson, directed by Shaw, toured in the play in the British provinces in 1900. This fine actor tried frequently to appear again as Dick in London, but after Shaw wrote the part of Caesar for him, he consistently side-tracked the actor whenever the latter showed signs of wanting to play the lesser if flashier part.

Pre-24. Bright Inserts a Notice by Himself to Explain Shaw's Next Letter

---

THE LAND OF LETTERS

The Gospel of "G.B.S."

A Revolting and Dehumanising Document.

"If my readers do their fair share of the work, I daresay they will understand nearly as much of the plays as I do myself"—thus does Mr. Bernard Shaw encouragingly pat the public on the back, anticipating its contortions and discomforts, as he thrusts the formidable pill of his "Plays: Pleasant and Unpleasant" (two vols. London: Grant Richards) down its throat. The apologia was not unneeded, for this author's works are assuredly not for all markets—indeed, it is difficult to determine for whom he is purveying, since even "the happy prisoners of the home," revolting daughters to whom he claims to be the bearer of a message, may turn and rend the new evangelist for his caricatures of themselves. One fears, however, that the reverse may be the case, for the majority of women fatten on men's lies, and the liar whom they take to their hearts with the greatest fervour is he who, professing loudly that he understands the sex and the motives governing its actions, betrays every indication of never having passed the outposts. Where, for instance, has Mr. Shaw met the originals of Blanche Sartorius, Vivie Warren, Raina Petkoff, and Louka, the bloodless creations of his own ratiocinative temperament? He may call them types of the advanced woman of today, but they are not, as he will find when he looks outside in the world for his material and not within.

.   .   .

Again, in regard to his male characters, Mr. Shaw may be "the voice of one crying in the wilderness," heralding the advent of some new Messiah, but his words fall meaninglessly to the ground because his ideas are expressed in insoluble terms of his own personality. "To be intelligible is to be found out," he may retort in the words of a fellow Irishman and wit, but the pertinacious presentment of himself as protagonist of each and all his works does not make for drama, but for sheer boredom and extinction.

.   .   .

The brain which can, in the course of five years, evolve seven plays of serious import by way of recreation from heavier work is, one unhesitatingly admits, abnormal; the pity is that, with such opportunities and talents, Mr. Shaw should have elected to contrive everything in the same unpleasing mould of acrimonious psychology. He comes into the dramatic arena singularly well equipped for the fray; he has a quick eye for striking situations, he is gifted with humour, wit, invention, and a power of expression of a very high order, but—fatal but!—he has no deep sympathy with humanity at large, and his overweening love of paradox leads him to see through the wrong end of the telescope. In all his plays, with one exception (with which I shall deal presently), there is nothing helpful, nothing stimulating to the heart; all is as drear and unsatisfying as the arid waste of the desert. And, though it is futile to expect idealism from one who is at no pains to conceal his contempt for it, we have at least the right to demand of the realist that he shall be artistic in his methods, which Mr. Shaw, unfortunately, is not. However true it might be of Mr. Wells's tentacular Martians, it is certainly false of average men and women to define their love either as an hysterical emotion or as a mere animal instinct dominated by sexual attraction; and Mr. Shaw, in insisting on these as the only points of view, betrays the narrowness of his observation and the superficiality of his reasoning.

.   .   .

I have no space to deal at length with each separate play, but the last word on "Arms and the Man" and "Widowers' Houses" was spoken at the time of their production. Of the rest, "The Philanderer" is unspeakably nauseous, both in thought and expression, and the author's smiling self-satisfaction, as he plunges his hands deeper and deeper into the moral cesspool, is not the least revolting side of the business. He is said, by the way, to have spoken of this work as "dull filth unfit for human consumption," and it would be hard to find a more apposite description. "Mrs. Warren's Profession," though dealing with a most revolting subject, is a work of such amazing vigour and extraordinary power as almost to stupefy the coolest-headed. Even in his strongest scene, however, Mr. Shaw has minimized the effect in characteristic fashion. This is Vivie's comment on hearing that her mother is a shameful procuress, with establishments in all the great Continental capitals:—

"My dear mother,—you are a wonderful woman—you are stronger than all England, and are you really and truly not one wee bit doubtful—or—or—ashamed?" Is this emotionless, sexless creature really typical of the true New Woman of today? I trow not, though Mr. Shaw is at such trouble to make her consistent in her cold-bloodedness. "The Man of Destiny" is a prolix elaboration of familiar materials, the author having dramatised the quintessence of Taine's "Modern Régime." Napoleon's boast to Madame de Clermont-Tonnerre, "I'm always living two years in advance," is however, scarcely justification for enabling him to foresee the rotten state of the English labour market in 1898, and his conviction of the Church Missionary Society, the capitalists, and the Forward politicians of today has apparently wandered into the play from some Fabian pamphlet. "You Never Can Tell" is as impossible, but not so skilful, as "Arms and the Man"—impossible, that is, in the strange admixture of drama, high comedy, and farce. The alternations from one to the other are as wonderful as a kaleidoscope, but the result on the mind of the reader is bewilderment and chaos.

.   .   .

There remains "Candida," and, for the sake of its purity and strength, one would willingly forget the remaining works—good, bad and indifferent. It is because Mr. Shaw has, for once, not been ashamed to figure as a man of sentiment that he has succeeded in writing a really beautiful play where he failed before through excess of brainishness. In Candida he has depicted the real product of the New Woman movement—a noble-minded, graceful woman of dignity and resource, strong where her husband is weak, a Christian Socialist. The author's reasons for making the Rev. J. M. Morell, active member of the C.S.U., the Guild of St. Matthew, etc., a weak-kneed, windbag rhetorician are not obvious, but in every other respect the play is quite a faultless work of art. If only Mr. Shaw would give himself up more frequently to this mood, the reproach that we have no serious drama in England would soon be a gibe of the past.

.   .   .

But which way do his thoughts naturally tend? "It was as Punch that I emerged from obscurity," he tells his readers in one of his diverting prefaces, and they may be driven to the belief that he prefers to go down to posterity in the same role. Certainly they will not lack material for this view, since, within a few pages of each other, he has made elaborate defences of such parasites on the modern drama as the Censor of Plays and the actor-manager. After that, he who would pluck out the heart of Mr. Shaw's mystery must own himself beaten, but no one can afford to neglect the attempt. These plays, both in idea and treatment, inaugurate a new departure, and, if anyone should fear for their reception in the theatre, let him take comfort from the author's paradoxical assertion that "it is quite possible for a piece to enjoy the most sensational success on the basis of a complete misunderstanding of its philosophy." On this assumption a fortune should be in store for the manager who would hazard the production of any one of these plays—save "Candida."

R. G. B.

Bright was now obviously at least a contributor to a column in *The Sun* called "The Land of Letters." Possibly it was his own column. Unfortunately this piece is not dated; Shaw's letter, which follows, refers to it, but is dated December 15th. It seems hardly likely that Bright, who has now dropped his second initial and signs himself R. G. B., would have waited until the end of the year to review the volumes which appeared in the spring. . . . Bright's question concerning the originals of Shaw's women characters was, granted, rhetorical, but he might have been surprised had Shaw told him that Blanche Sartorius (*Widowers' Houses*) was modeled upon Shaw's actress-friend Florence Farr and a woman he saw on the street one night (see the anecdote as told by himself in Pearson, *Portrait*, pp. 162-163), and Vivie Warren was modeled upon a young girl Shaw knew, Susan Lawrence, whose career and character Shaw reproduced, even to her cigars, in Vivie—he did not, however, give Vivie Susan's monocle. Louka and Raina, apparently, were pure creations, a fair enough balance in *Arms and the Man*, since Bluntschli was patterned after Sidney Webb and Sergius after Cunningham Grahame, two of Shaw's best friends. Florence Farr most certainly would have been startled and probably blazingly angry at being called a "bloodless creation" of Shaw's "ratiocinative temperament" (a vile phrase!), and one suspects even the efficient young cigar-smoking and monocle-wearing Newnham graduate might have protested. . . . The epigram in the second paragraph with a prefatory "Now-a-days" in the original is spoken by Lord Darlington in the first act of Oscar Wilde's *Lady Winder-*

mere's Fan (1892). . . . Bright's accusation that Shaw's protagonists all represented himself is still made in the mid-fifties by those who do not or cannot read the plays really carefully. Good Shavians know that even in the earliest plays Shaw was one of the truly great creators of dramatic characters. If it is true that in almost every play at least one character does present ideas his creator believed in, it is indisputable that his interest in debate and dialectic always made him present other characters who had equally good arguments for the opposition. Of the philanderer Charteris, for instance, Shaw once told Archibald Henderson: "Charteris is as much myself as Berowne, Mercutio and Benedick are Shakespeare. They are all cads, if you like, just as Charteris has been called a cad; but does that really dispose of them?" . . . "Acrimonious psychology" just *might* apply to certain scenes or characters in the "Unpleasant" plays, but certainly not to anything in the "Pleasant" ones. Young Golding, possibly self-conscious about his debt to his patron, was trying just a bit too hard to be Bright. . . . Considering the amount of quite gratuitous help of all kinds which the young man had been receiving for four years, it is a shock to discover him accusing Shaw of possessing "no deep sympathy with humanity at large." The point of view is so puzzle-headed that there is no point in arguing it here. . . . I cannot think of anything truly "stimulating to the heart," even in *Candida* where Bright found it, but to label even the "Unpleasant" plays "drear and unsatisfying as the arid waste of the desert" is singularly imperceptive and indeed shockingly suggestive of a whole arid waste of blind spots in the critic. . . . H. G. Wells's "tentacular Martians" Bright had met in *The War of the Worlds,* probably just published. . . . It was somewhat cavalier of the critic to write "the last word on 'Arms and the Man' and 'Widowers' Houses' was spoken at the time of their production," since the first play, except from himself, won instant and definite approval, and the second was, at best, a *succès de scandale.* . . . *The Philanderer* is certainly not one of Shaw's better plays, but it is not nearly so bad as Bright suggests; Shaw's comment on the play quoted in the fourth paragraph may remind the reader that in the long letter of June 10, 1896, the author had called *The Philanderer* "vulgar and immoral and cynically disrespectful of ladies and gentlemen." William Archer had taken the play when first written as almost a personal insult and said he felt like cutting his good friend in public for having perpetrated such an "outrage upon art and decency." Hesketh Pearson, in a typically vague passage, records that some time in 1896 Shaw read the play to some friends and found it, three years after composition, "a combination of mechanical farce with realistic filth which quite disgusted" him. Obviously Bright and Pearson refer to the same comment; it is quite typical that the wording differs. . . . Shaw, normally determined to cite his sources and positively loquacious about them, to my knowledge never mentioned Taine in connection with *The Man of Destiny*. Hippolyte Taine (1828–1893), French historian and critic, is known to English-speaking readers mainly for his *History of English Literature* in the translation of Van Laun of 1893. In the letter which follows, Shaw attempts to straighten Bright out on some of the latter's comments on this play, but does not mention Taine. . . . If Bright misread *Candida*, one can only murmur, "Who hasn't?" and the answer would have to be, "Very few, indeed, even among professed and advanced Shavians." Anyway, in the June 10, 1896, letter, Shaw, without stressing his irony, if implying it in the end-phrase, had encouraged the misreading by calling the play "the poetry of the Wife and Mother—the Virgin Mother in the true sense, & so on & so forth." . . . Morell is described by Shaw as "an active member of the Guild of St. Matthew and the Christian Social Union."

24. Shaw Comments on Bright's Review and Provides More Gossip

15th Dec. 1898.

Telegraph Office: Grayshott, Hants.   Blen-Cathra, Hindhead,
Railway Station: Haslemere 3¼ miles.   Haslemere, Surrey.

Dear Mr. Bright

I was just wondering, when your letter came, whether it would be safe to send you a Wagnerite to your old address. I gather, however, that you have read that work. I wanted to send it because I thought a review which appeared in the Sun of my plays, signed R.G.B., a very promising one. Some of my "unpleasant" achievements horrified you a little; and the fact that the feeling insisted on finding expression, and apt and forcible expression, when you would have probably rather liked to be complimentary, convinced me that you had not mistaken your profession. Of course I didn't share your view of the plays: if I did, I should destroy them promptly; but that, you will understand, is not the point. The thing is that having something to say, you said it effectively, and got as far as a column without being superfluous. Further, you pitched into an author without offending him, a thing that can only be done by saying your mind quite sincerely. No doubt you have by this time found out for yourself that you can handle the pen a bit; but it is always worth knowing how far that impression has been made on another party.

By the way, Napoleon's allusion to Manchester cotton is no anachronism. It would be one if made by Kitchener to-day; but at the beginning of the century the new cotton factories of the industrial revolution were horrible dens of child slavery; and Napoleon had heard all about them quite in the S.D.F. manner at the Jacobin clubs which he frequented in Paris before he got his chance at Toulon. You have no idea how old the ultra-modern revolutionary platform always is—indeed the political platform generally. In my Caesar & Cleopatra, when it is published, you will find apparently outrageous gags in the aspect of allusions to the foreign politics of the Beaconsfield-Salisbury period, which are nevertheless as "historical" as anything in Addison's "Cato."

I have no information to give you beyond this: that the play and The Perfect Wagnerite have been produced under great difficulties owing to my illness & my chapter of accidents. However, the play is now finished, except for the final revision and the arrangement of the stage business, at which I am at work now at the cost of a serious loss of ground in my recovery. It is in five acts, containing eight scenes, & involving considerable

variety and splendor of mounting. It begins with the arrival of
Caesar in Egypt in pursuit of Pompey after the battle of Phar-
salia, & ends with his departure after his six months stay in
Alexandria with Cleopatra. The whole episode was rejected by
Froude as a mere romance; but Mommsen describes it in considerable detail. The famous episode of the carpet in which
Appolodorus the Sicilian conveyed Cleopatra into Caesar's
presence is introduced; but in a way which would considerably
astonish the French painters who are so fond of the subject.

Nothing whatever has been settled as to the performance of
the play. Of course Caesar & Cleopatra suggests Forbes Robertson & Mrs. Patrick Campbell; but they are not responsible for
this, nor am I. I have read the first act alone to some friends in
private, but to no one else. All announcements as to the destina-
tion of the play are premature: nothing has been proposed,
nothing is pending. I shall take no trouble to get the play performed, as I shall be busy enough with its successor, which,
with "The Devil's Disciple" and C. & C., will form my next
volume of plays, & will certainly be published without any
delay on the chance of production.

It seems an indispensable condition of my recovery that I
should stop working. Yet I cannot escape. I must finish the
play completely before the end of the year. Then I have an
Italian Essay to write. Then a third play to complete my
volume.

When you tell me of recovering in six weeks from a fall of
50 ft. & a broken leg, I can only envy you. My left foot has
been hanging useless, with a hole in the instep, for 8 months, &
seems likely to complete the year, at least.

Put any of this information that you may care to use in your
own words as usual.

In haste (my wife being exceedingly angry with me for
writing after dinner)
                                    Yrs faithfully
                                    G. Bernard Shaw.

Whether or not Bright asked for a copy of *The Perfect Wagnerite*, he did review it in "The Land of Letters" column in *The Sun*, as the next entry here shows. The volume, subtitled *A Commentary on the Niblung's Ring*, was published by Grant Richards in 1898. . . . Again one must stress Shaw's fair-mindedness and generosity; however much he disagreed with Bright's criticism, he tends rather to overpraise his critical judgment and his style, and corrects him only on matters of fact. . . . Horatio Herbert Kitchener had become in 1898 the great British hero by recapturing Khartoum, the capital of the Anglo-Egyptian Sudan. . . . S. D. F., as noted before, refers to Hyndman's Social-Democratic Foundation. . . . In this letter Shaw mentions for the first time *Caesar and Cleopatra*, the play which he wrote for Johnston Forbes Robertson's "heroic" style of acting. . . . The statesman whose name he linked with Disraeli's was Robert Arthur Talbot Gascoyne, 3rd Marquis of Salisbury (1830–1903). . . . Joseph Addison's cold and classical tragedy, *Cato* (1713), was so filled with topical references that it was hailed by both Whigs and Tories as political propaganda for their sides. . . . Shaw's "illness" was caused by a foot-infection, which climaxed a general breakdown caused by his work upon the play and the book mentioned, his weekly reviews, and his political, Vestryman, and Fabian duties. . . . James Anthony Froude (1818–1894) was historian, editor of *Fraser's Magazine* (1860–1874), Regius Professor of Modern History at Oxford (1892–1894), friend, literary executor, and biographer of Carlyle, and writer of many works on history. Theodor Mommsen (1817–1903), German historian and archaeologist, published his most celebrated work, *Roman History*, in 1854–1856; Shaw relied upon him heavily for his ideas on Caesar, as the preface to that play proves. . . . In the play Shaw spelled the name of the dashing young Sicilian merchant Apollodorus. . . . The first professional production of the play, under the direction of Max Reinhardt, was in Berlin, March 31, 1906. Forbes Robertson did not play the part written for him until October 30th of that same year, at the Amsterdam Theatre, New York. In September of 1907, he played it at the Grand Theatre, Leeds, and under the management of Vedrenne and Barker at the Savoy, London, opening November 25. Both in America and England Cleopatra was played by Forbes

Robertson's wife, Gertrude Elliott. To many of us it seems unfortunate that Mrs. Pat, for whom the play was written almost as much as for Shaw's favorite "Heroic Actor," appeared in the play only once, when her touring company, including Nutcombe Gould, Courtney Thorpe, and Granville-Barker, gave the copyright performance at the Theatre Royal, Newcastle-upon-Tyne, March 15, 1899. . . . Shaw mentions this play's "successor"; although obviously not yet started in actual writing, this was *Captain Brassbound's Conversion*, written for Ellen Terry (the part of Lady Cicely Waynflete), and published, with *The Devil's Disciple* and the Caesar play, in 1901 as *Three Plays for Puritans*. . . . Frankly, I have no idea to what the "Italian Essay" refers; I have never seen even mention of any publication by Shaw which the description would fit. . . . The first mention here of Shaw's wife may startle the reader; Shaw had met Charlotte Payne-Townshend, a wealthy Irishwoman, at the summer home of Sidney and Beatrice Webb in 1896, a meeting definitely and deliberately arranged by Mrs. Webb. He began writing about her to Ellen Terry almost immediately; by the beginning of 1898 the friendship had progressed to the point where she served both as secretary and nurse to Shaw; when the infected foot developed first into an abscess in his instep and then into necrosis of the bone, Miss Payne-Townshend took him firmly in hand, and since Shaw objected to a church wedding, they were married on June 1, 1898, at the West Strand Registry office. The marriage proved certainly one of the happiest and most successful recorded of a major English man of letters. Charlotte managed her husband magnificently until her sudden death on September 12, 1943.

Post-24. Bright Inserts His Review of
The Perfect Wagnerite

THE LAND OF LETTERS

"THE PERFECT WAGNERITE"
and some imperfections.

"How dost thou, Benedick, the married man?" We all know the crushing and witty retort of Signor Mountanto to Don Pedro, and Mr. Bernard Shaw's reply to the same (though unspoken) question will soon be as familiar. Under the comprehensive title of "The Perfect Wagnerite" he has contrived, amongst other things, a subtle, but cogent and glowing, panegyric of love as the noblest impulse in life, the crown of all earthly achievements. Of love the destroyer, love returned upon itself and blighting the possessor, he recks nothing. For him "God's in his Heaven—all's well with the world," and that suffices. The doctrine is old, prehistoric almost; but, emanating from a chartered cynic, whose fiercest diatribes have been directed against it in the past, it derives added weight. What a chastening effect it has had on the author, and on his style. "Where be your gibes now? Your flashes of merriment that were wont to set the table in a roar?" He who was used to rail at and contemn conventions is become their very slave; and his explanation of "Das Rheingold," through the medium of a delicious little allegory about "a young and good-looking woman" at Klondike before the gold fever set in, is a charmingly optimistic conceit after the best manner of Mr. Ruskin. That it should come to this! But, perhaps, I do wrong to take the cynic's conversion seriously. After all, adulation is the subtlest form of abuse, and this glorification of love and the married state may be the merest subterfuge. You never can tell with this author.

. . .

"This book is a commentary on 'The Ring of the Niblungs,' Wagner's chief work. I offer it to those enthusiastic admirers of Wagner who are unable to follow his ideas, and do not in the least understand the dilemma of Wotan, though they are filled with indignation at the irreverence of the Phillistines who frankly avow that they find the remarks of the god too often tedious and nonsensical." Having defined his position thus clearly, Mr. Shaw proceeds to envelop the hapless enthusiasts in still more impenetrable fogs of doubt and bewilderment. He becomes "all things to all men"—though scarcely in the apostolic sense. To those in search of knowledge he is (professedly) a guide, philosopher, and friend; over the superior person he exercises superiority; upon the adept musician he pours out his vial of merciless scorn and contempt. You may have had the temerity to regard "The Ring" as the embodiment, in dramatic form, of sagas which the genius of Mr. William Morris cast in romantic moulds. If so, you are anathema to Mr. Shaw, whose least contemptuous definition of you is "ignoramus". After this, you will scarcely be surprised to find that, not only was Wagner an exiled revolutionist, but that his aim throughout his work was philosophically symbolic. And then—inevitably—are evolved from the dead man's brain philippics against greed of gold, "dangerous trades", established authority, statesmen, the survival of the unfittest, the application of the criminal code, Bryant and May's match factories, clerical shareholders in the same, "phossy jaw", and what not. For further points, vide labour leaders' speeches, passim. In fact, Wagner and his works are nothing more than a convenient wall behind which Mr. Shaw ensconces himself, and hurls forth a Fabian essay of characteristic acumen and violence. The position is smilingly given away by the author's naive reference, for further enlightenment, to his Fabian Society tract, "The Impossibilities of

Anarchism". The worst of your Socialistic propagandist is his inveterate habit of establishing ethical signification in the work of every man whose cause he champions. The lengths to which this may go have recently been demonstrated by the publication of "The Tempter". One person, at least, is in no doubt as to the ethical signfication underlying that niggling piece of blasphemous rhodomontade—Mr. Henry Arthur Jones, to wit. Mr. Shaw's polemics are all very dazzling, but is it Wagner? And are the difficulties of comprehension met by the knowledge that Alberic is not only a dwarf by birth, but in brain, typifying the millionaire capitalist, the sweating employer of labour, the foolhardy company promoter; Siegfried, the saviour of Society; Wotan, the ruler exercising dominion over credulous fools by sheer force of circumstance—not of birthright? The promise of elucidation is delusive, after all.

But, though Mr. Shaw, as I have tried to show, had veiled a strong indictment against Society under a delusive title, he is not wanting in new ideas on the sempiternal question of Wagner's intentions. Quite the most daring of these is his contention that "Die Götterdämmerung" is a thorough grand opera, in support of which he adduces internal evidence to prove that, although played as the last of the tetralogy, it was in reality conceived first. The apple of discord he cheerily casts into the musical arena, and smilingly awaits the dilemma of some new Paris. Heaven forbid that I should pick it up! Mr. Shaw says the last word on the vexed point—was Brynhild ravished on the mountain-side, and, if so, by whom?—though sentimentalists will view with alarm the restoration of her virginity at the price of perjury and murder. He also advances Wagner's explanation of his own work, which, however, necessarily falls short of G.B.S.'s, and, in conclusion, pleads strongly for the establishment of a Wagner Theatre and Festival in London. This is, indeed, one of his few moments of earnestness in the whole book. May one hope that in his next book Mr. Shaw will descend still further towards his public? To pile an Ossa of bewilderment upon a Pelion of mystification baffles and disheartens the student, who would understand his tutor, if only the latter were more considerate in his use of a superior intellect. Meantime, no professing Wagnerite—and who in these days is not?—can afford to neglect this commentary on "The Ring." It may upset preconceived ideas, and occasionally annoy the reader by sheer force of egoism; but, as a piece of well-reasoned criticism, it does for music what Mr. Ruskin did for Turner in "Modern Painters," and it is written in Mr. Shaw's most brilliant and attractive style.

R. G. B.

"Signior Mountanto" is Beatrice's first reference to Benedick, in the first scene of *Much Ado About Nothing.* Benedick's "crushing and witty retort" to Don Pedro's question, at the close of the play, is a long prose paragraph; probably Bright was thinking particularly of this sentence: "In brief, since I do propose to marry, I will think nothing to any purpose that the world can say against it; and therefore never flout at me for what I have said against it; for man is a giddy thing, and this is my conclusion." . . . Golding Bright is, so far as I know, the only critic ever to have found the very Shavian volume on Wagner's *Ring*-cycle a "panegyric of love" occasioned by his own marriage. It is a provocative, if not at all a probable, interpretation. . . . Bright's agile memory took a sudden jump from the relevant *Much Ado* lines (which Bright condensed) to the skull of Yorick: "Where be your jibes now? your gambols? your songs? your flashes of merriment, that were wont to set the table on a roar?" . . . Nevertheless, the whole of the first paragraph, for us who realize the personal relationship between reviewer and reviewed, is a pleasant enough bit of spoofing, even to the pun in the last sentence. . . . The "delicious little allegory" of the girl at Klondyke (Shaw's spelling) will be found by the curious in the first two paragraphs of "The Rhine Gold" analysis. It is too long for quotation, too compact for summarizing. . . . In the chapter entitled "Wagner as Revolutionist," after citing considerable data upon the composer's political beliefs and actions which led to his being publicly proclaimed "a politically dangerous person," Shaw did indeed write that anyone who accused him of reading *his* Socialistic ideas into the opera book of a "dilettantist" could "safely be dismissed . . . as an ignoramus." Bright's paraphrase, obviously, was too generalized here. . . . Was it not somewhat inconsistent of Bright to find *The Perfect Wagnerite* at once a "panegyric of love as the noblest impulse in life" and "a Fabian essay of characteristic acumen and violence"? . . . In a sub-section entitled "Anarchism no Panacea" of an ideological chapter, "Siegfried as Protestant," following the analytical third chapter on the third play of the cycle, Shaw referred disciples of Siegfried to his own Fabian Tract #45, *The Impossibilities of Anarchism*, read to the Fabian Society October 16, 1891, and published July, 1893. . . . Shaw's good if frequently captious friend, Henry Arthur Jones, had, several years earlier, written a four-act tragedy in blank verse, *The Tempter*, which Beerbohm Tree had presented at the Haymarket September 20, 1893. It met a very mixed reception when produced; it ran seventy nights, but was a financial failure. It had just been published when Bright wrote (in November 1898, Macmillan's), and had contained a preface in which Jones defended his play and specifically attacked William Archer for his review of the production. Shaw wrote a letter to Jones on December 2, 1898, with one paragraph on this play, "a most amazing frisk," "Altogether a rum business," but "a *tour-de-force* and a lesson to the accursed literary amateur," containing in its verse "a model of speakability"—very high praise, indeed, from Shaw. A month later he wrote to Jones, January 8, 1899, a long and very interesting letter obviously in answer to Jones's comments on the Wagner volume. (See Doris Arthur Jones's biography of her father, *Taking the Curtain Call*, pp. 117-124.) Just why, except that the play had recently been published, Bright should have dragged in the author of *The Tempter* as an apparent example of "your Socialistic propagandist" is today to a student of the period an insoluble mystery. . . . The last two sentences of the concluding paragraph make splendid amends for what might seem to some of us familiar with *The Perfect Wagnerite* a somewhat over-critical review.

25. From Shipboard Shaw Keeps His Young Protégé Posted

POST CARD

Post marked
Alger Oct., '99.
London Oc. 26. '99.

R. Golding Bright,
Author's Club,
3, Whitehall Court,
London, S.W.

L'Angleterre.

23rd October, 1899.
S. S. Luzinatia.

I have left Hindhead: please cancel that address and fall back on 29 Fitzroy Square W or 10 Adelphi Terrace W.C. Nothing is settled about the D's D: M.C. only had my license to perform it at Kennington until my return on the 30th inst. I am not in any attitude about it: it is available for any manager who wants it. Yes: "Captain Brassbound's Conversion" is the third play I mentioned to you. It was written for Ellen Terry, not for Sir H.I.; and she will possibly produce it independently; but this is not to be taken as indicating any rupture at the Lyceum. Miss Achurch asked Harvey to play the poet in Candida, not Morell. He refused. Forbes Robertson is not going to produce "Caesar". He had the refusal up to last May, when he definitely decided not to venture on it. But as you know, all these decisions mean as little as the opposite decisions which give rise to them. You may safely contradict every statement you see in print about my plays. They are all nonsense.

G. Bernard Shaw.

FOR INFORMATION ABOUT THE STAGE SOCIETY, APPLY TO FREDERICK WHELEN CARE OF GRANT RICHARDS, 9 HENRIETTA ST. COVENT GARDEN.

Shaw did not like foreign travel, although as a bachelor he did visit Bayreuth several times and Zurich for the International Socialist Congress. But Charlotte loved to travel and the Shaws took the first of several voyages together late in 1899, a Mediterranean trip to Athens, Villefranche, Syracuse, and Algiers. On the same day that Shaw wrote to Bright, his wife wrote to Grant Richards that he was bored with "the confinement of the ship's life," and that they both looked forward to returning to London. . . . Notice that Shaw implies a prompt return. The "D's D" is *The Devil's Disciple*; M. C. is Murray Carson. Here Shaw first names *Captain Brassbound's Conversion*, which, like so many of his earlier plays, had to wait several years before it was produced as he wished. While on tour with Irving earlier during this month, on October 9th, Ellen Terry had given the copyright performance at the Court Theatre, Liverpool, October 10, 1899, using members of the Lyceum company and with Laurence Irving as Brassbound. In December, 1900, the Stage Society presented Janet Achurch and young Irving for two performances in London. Janet and her husband (as Sir Howard Hallem) were presented for six performances at the Queen's Theatre, Manchester, by Harold V. Neilson, who played Brassbound, in May, 1902. Finally Vedrenne and Barker presented Ellen Terry in the part written for her at the Royal Court for six matinées beginning March 20, 1906. In this production Captain Kearney was played by a young American actor, James Carew, who became Ellen's third husband. Shaw originally called the play *The Witch of Atlas*; later he considered *The Angel*

of Atlas, "or some such silliness," but finally settled upon "the ugly but arresting name" which the play was to bear. Ellen's and Shaw's letters from May 31, 1899, through February 9, 1900, are largely concerned with the play and the possibility of her appearing as Lady Cicely. In December, 1900, the actress began inquiring about the Stage Society production with Janet Achurch; at the performance, at the Strand Theatre, December 16, after corresponding with each other since June, 1892, actress and author met each other—under the stage—for the first time. The only reference made to the meeting was in a note from Ellen dated December 10, 1902. Sporadically from February 22, 1906, through April 25, 1908 (the letters by this time had dwindled to an average of three a year), the play again cropped up in the Terry-Shaw correspondence, first with reference to the Royal Court production (Shaw sent her some pointed coaching advice), and with an American and later a British tour with her new husband in a repertory which included *Captain Brassbound's Conversion.* . . . The reference to Janet Achurch and *Candida,* in view of the "asked," must refer to her provincial tour with that play in 1897; she was to play it for the Stage Society at the Strand, July 1, 1900, but would hardly have been assembling her support so early. Harvey was to become Sir John Martin-Harvey, actor-manager famous for constant revivals of *The Only Way,* a dramatization of Dickens' *A Tale of Two Cities.* One of Irving's many juveniles who were to become famous in their own right, he left the Lyceum company in 1897 and began free-lancing. . . . Miss Achurch's Marchbanks on tour was Courtney Thorpe; at the Strand in 1900 Granville-Barker, as we have previously noted. The Stage Society, a private subscription club, was founded in 1899 by Frederick Whelen, a cousin of Grant Richards, and eventually an assistant in management to Beerbohm Tree. Its first production, November 26, 1899, was *You Never Can Tell,* the first Sunday performance in England since the time of Charles II. The cast was a strong one, including Yorke Stephens, the original Blunstschli; Hermann Vezin, an "old school" actor whom Shaw much admired; James Welch, the original Lickcheese, who directed; and Charles Charrington, husband of Janet Achurch and the original Morell. . . . Obviously what looks like a postscript in full caps is a printed note at the foot of the stationery Shaw was using. . . . By 1905 The Stage Society was to present Janet Achurch in *Candida* and *Captain Brassbound's Conversion,* Fanny Brough in *Mrs. Warren's Profession* and *The Admirable Bashville,* and Granville-Barker, Lewis Casson, Lillah McCarthy and Edmund Gwenn in *Man and Superman.*

26. Bright Is Posted on the Latest Shaw
Developments and Advised on His Own Career

10, Adelphi Terrace, W.C.
2nd May, 1900.

Dear Bright

The Three Plays for Puritans will be published next autumn. There will be quite a collection of prefaces, chief among them a tremendous sermon entitled "Why for Puritans." In it I give, with exceeding frankness, an account of the London Theatres as I found them during my critical campaign on the Saturday Review from 1895 to 1898, when I collapsed and nearly died of pure inanity and emptiness administered by the managers in large weekly doses. I appeal, of course, to the Puritans to come to the rescue of the stage; and to shew that this is no mere personal eccentricity of mine—no hackneyed Shawism—I find, whilst my preface is still in MS, William Archer in the Morning Leader, crying out for a new Collier to write a new treatise on "the profaneness & immorality &c," and Massingham immediately afterwards hotly defending George Moore against Walkley from the Puritan point of view.

In a second preface I attack the current critical chatter about the so-called originality of my plays, shewing that the peculiar Diabolonian creed of the Devil's Disciple is as old as William

Blake, and had been freshly affirmed by Robert Buchanan in a poem published before the D's D was written; that the contrast between mere knighthood and military capacity which is the theme of Arms & The Man was elaborated years ago in Mommsen's History of Rome, one of the best known books in Europe; that Buchanan was quite right in pointing out that my stage tricks are as old as Charles Mathews in Cool as a Cucumber, & probably centuries older; and that, in short, it is only the criticism that reads nothing, remembers nothing, and knows nothing, that is astonished and bewildered by my sallies.

A third preface deals with Shakespear, and with epoch making authors and artists in general, explaining my view that Shakespear's epoch is over.

I have not yet written any more prefaces; so it only remains to say that the book will conclude with an appendix consisting of the three plays—The Devil's Disciple, Caesar & Cleopatra, and Captain Brassbound's Conversion. Publishers: Grant Richards and H. S. Stone & co. of Chicago.

Now as to yourself. Your danger is not failing to get work, but getting too much. Journalism, when it gets hold of a willing & capable horse, walks him to death at forty, and leaves his ghost walking painfully for another twenty or thirty. All you can do, of course, is to blaze away; but in as far as you can economize yourself, do. Editorships, which are the prizes of the profession, are frightfully precarious—witness the case of Massingham. Try and fire off a book or two, or get a personal hold of the public in some way, unless you become as strong in the special journalist's art of knowing the public and picking the writers as to be unassailable.

In haste

yrs ever

G. Bernard Shaw.

On May 14, 1898, Shaw, physically worn out, announced his retirement as *Saturday Review* drama critic ("G.B.S. Vivisected") and the following week closed his career with his "Valedictory" and named his successor, "the incomparable Max" Beerbohm, younger brother to the actor-manager Beerbohm Tree. . . . Note the first appearance of the term "Shawism" in the letters. (A. B. Walkley had used the word in his review of the 1894 *Arms and the Man*, but not in the sense of an idiosyncratic statement, rather for Shaw's comic method as opposed to "Gilbertism.") Charles Archer in his bibliography of his brother's work did not list the *Morning Leader* article. . . . Jeremy Collier, non-juring clergyman, in 1698 published the most famous attack upon the Restoration drama of Congreve, Vanbrugh, Wycherley, and Dryden, *A Short View of the Immorality and Profaneness of the English Stage*. . . . H. W. Massingham, famous journalist and editor of *The Star, The Daily Chronicle* and *The Nation*, Shaw had known and admired since the eighties. To a selection of his writings, edited by his son, H. J., in 1925, Shaw was to contribute an appreciation, reprinted in his own *Pen Portraits and Reviews* (1931). . . . Robert Buchanan, poet, novelist, critic, and playwright, mainly famous for his attack upon the pre-Raphaelites in "The Fleshly School of Poetry," was active in his various fields of writing from 1866 through 1895. He died in 1901. The poem referred to was "The Devil's Case. Now for the First Time Correctly Stated, and Diligently Versified, as a Bank Holiday Interlude" (1894). . . . Charles James Mathews, famous light comedian of the sixties and seventies, was famous mainly for his portrayal of Plumper in a trivial farce by Blanchard Jerrold, *Cool as a Cucumber*, first produced at the Lyceum April 29, 1850. Translated into French as *Un Anglais Timide*, it was also played by Mathews for nearly a month at the Théâtre des Variéties in Paris. He was the husband of the famous comedienne, Madame Vestris, "The Witch of Wych Street." . . . The "third preface," to *Caesar and Cleopatra*, was ironically to cause Shaw much unfair and rather ignorant criticism, since from 1901 until the present most alleged critics have preferred to overlook the question mark in "Better than Shakespeare?" in the title. . . . After a long period during which he had been concerned mainly with "feeding" Bright with material for his column, Shaw again offers some sane personal advice.

27. More Material for the Gossip Column

10, Adelphi Terrace, W.C.
2nd November 1900.

Dear Golding Bright

Now that the Borough Council election is over, I can snatch a moment to answer your letter. "Three Plays for Puritans" is passed for press at last, though the effort has almost slain me; for you will observe that I have had not only to fight the municipal election, but to write "Fabianism & the Empire" in the throes of the General Election before that. I have had, I need hardly say, no holiday. But the elections are over at last (though demands for speeches in connexion with the School Board & County Council elections are dropping in already); and the book is only waiting for the printing of the American edition and the reproduction of an Italian photograph of the mosaic in St. Marks representing the lighthouse of Alexandria. That is, of course, for Caesar & Cleopatra. There will also be a portrait of Caesar from the Berlin bust (our famous British Museum one has been given up at last as unconnected with Caesar), and a portrait of General Burgoyne (for the Devil's Disciple). Just observe, if you please, what these volumes mean. A play costs two or three times as much real work as a novel, which involves nothing but inkslinging. Yet I give an ungrateful public three plays in a volume, besides prefaces, notes & sermons without end. When I say give I mean give; for the book will not yield me dock laborer's wages for the mere manual toil it costs. This one has really three prefaces entitled respectively "Why for Puritans?", a criticism of the contemporary theatre, "On Diabolonian

Ethics" explaining the foundation of "The Devil's Disciple", and "Better than Shakespeare?" in which I clear up all that confusion to which you allude about Greek methods & Shakespear's epoch & so on.

Captain Brassbound's Conversion will be produced privately by the Stage Society in December if it can be cast—an open question at present. The Devil's Disciple is coining money in the provinces in the hands of Forbes Robertson: its production in Dublin the other day seems to have been furorious.

No more news at present: I do not even know yet whether I am elected for the Borough Council or not. If not, the relief will be enormous, and the dramatic output of next year a good deal bigger.

yrs sincerely
G. Bernard Shaw.

In 1900, having served three years as Vestryman for St. Pancras, Shaw was elected a Borough Councillor, when the Vestry became a Borough, actually, as noted earlier, the same position. . . . *Fabianism and the Empire: A Manifesto by the Fabian Society. Edited by Bernard Shaw,* was published by Grant Richards. Although only the "Editor's Preface" is signed G. B. S., Shaw actually drafted the whole pronouncement of 101 pages on the South African War, and it was then circulated among the members and altered to accord insofar as posible with all comments submitted. The work as printed, however, represented largely Shaw's own opinion, which, to the surprise of many in and out of the Society, was pro-imperialism rather than pro-Boer. . . . I have not seen the original (1901) Grant Richards edition of *Three Plays for Puritans,* but the reliable and meticulous bibliographer Geoffrey H. Wells lists only two illustrations, a "portrait," obviously from its position that of Burgoyne, and "an illustration," which would be the reproduction of the Italian photograph Shaw mentions. The portrait of Caesar would seem, then, not to have been published. . . . The Stage Society did, as we have noted, sponsor two performances of the Brassbound play in December. . . . Despite the comment here about Forbes Robertson's success with *The Devil's Disciple* on tour, and although he himself directed the production, Shaw would not allow it to be brought into London, and as late as December, 1903, he wrote a long letter to the actor attempting to beguile him out of his desire to act Dick Dudgeon and into playing Caesar.

28. A Personal Answer to a Personal Protest

12th December 1900.

10, Adelphi Terrace, W.C.

Dear Bright

In St Pancras we prosecute disorderly houses with great assiduity; and I have handed your letter to our leading Purity man to stimulate him to further exertions.

But what is the use of all that, except to make brothels less noisy and policemen more heavily tipped? In St Pancras a railway porter's wife, to whom five shillings a week added to her husband's wages makes all the difference between plenty and penury, will do char work for that sum to make it the standard price of a woman's labor in the district. Imagine what that means to the single woman or the widow with children. Suppose you were a young woman and had to choose between such starvation for honest work and picking up a shilling in Alfred Place or five in the Euston Road, how would you feel towards people who were quite satisfied to sweat you for twelve hours for a shilling, but would not hear of their sons being "solicited"? Read "Mrs. Warren's Profession" again. Everybody should read it carefully through once a month. If they did, we should get something better than virtuous indignation brought to bear on the subject.

Three Plays for Puritans will not be out until January. No advance copies as yet. You shall have one when they are ready.

Yours ever
G. Bernard Shaw.

Golding Bright, still only in his mid-twenties, seems to have been a very moral young man and to have been complaining to his mentor about prostitutes soliciting on the streets and the brothels which employed or exploited them. He might have realized the pointed answer he would receive from the objectively ironic author of the still-banned *Mrs. Warren's Profession.* . . . The new volume of plays did appear in January.

29. Advice on Approaching Frank Harris

10, Adelphi Terrace, W.C.
5th April, 1901.

Dear Golding Bright

I had better not give you an introduction to Frank Harris: he is not accessible in that way (very few men are, by the way). You had much better go at him on your own account. Tell him what has befallen you on the other papers, and say that your only chance is to find a strong editor. He may not find it at all easy to pitch on a dramatic critic. At all events, there is no harm in trying, provided you don't try to force his hand with an introduction.

The address for the new paper is 64 Victoria Street S.W.—least he has just written to me about it from there.

I have no intention of returning to regular journalism—no time for it.

Just off to Provence to recruit: I haven't had even a Sunday off since Oct 99.

Yrs sincerely
G. Bernard Shaw.

Frank Harris's "new paper," which he founded and edited, was *The Candid Friend*. Shaw contributed an exceedingly interesting two-part autobiographical article, "Who I Am and What I Think," to the issues of May 11th and May 18th, reprinted in *Sixteen Self Sketches* (1949). . . . None of the biographers records a visit to Provence in 1901. . . . The use of "recruit" is unusual, but dictionaries do give as one meaning of the verb, used intransitively, "to recover health, strength." . . . "Just off" at least did not mean immediately, for the next letter is dated from Adelphi Terrace the following day.

30. On Andrew Carnegie and an Endowed Theatre

10, Adelphi Terrace, W.C.
6th April, 1901.

Dear Golding Bright

Your letter, addressed most absolutely to Hindhead (now two years out of date) has only just reached me. Here is what you want about Carnegie.

All I can say is that if Mr. Carnegie proposes to be guided by a committee of critics, actors, actresses, managers, and students of the stage, the sooner he is made a ward in Chancery and strictly looked after, the better. Probably what Mr. Carnegie really said was that the committee should <u>not</u> include any critic, actor, actress, manager, or proposed student of the stage. If Mr. Carnegie is a wise man, he will buy my three volumes of plays and read the prefaces very carefully. He will have to provide himself with some small change, however, as I do not issue a five-million-dollar edition. I refer him more particularly to the preface to Volume II, "Pleasant Plays", in which I shew how a preliminary experiment can be tried in a businesslike way by inviting a manager of established competence to undertake a series of performances of selected plays with a guarantee to protect him against pecuniary loss. This would provide the first thing wanted: a repertory, and a company. If any play produced under these conditions proved a great popular success, the manager could immediately transfer it to his ordinary popular program. Finally he might take a separate theatre, or build one, for the endowed repertory; and that theatre might possibly soon have a steady clientèle which would make it independent of any guarantee. In Mr. Carnegie's place, I should make this proposition to Mr. Alexander in London and Mr. Mansfield in the United States, and see how it worked for a season or two. I repeat, it might prove so successful that a permanent endowment would be quite unnecessary—that a start is all that is required.

For permanent endowment, I should reserve such a scheme as Mr. Alexander has suggested, of a school of physical expression and rhetoric attached to the London University, and available for the personal training of clergymen, barristers, naval and military officers, and all persons who have to speak or command in public, including, of course, actors, but no more specialized for actors than for theologians or jurists. The first qualification I require from an actor is that he shall be able to impress the back row of the gallery with his speech and bearing; and that is what the captain of a P. & O. steamer requires also from his third officer. And there are a hundred departments of business in which this personal training is as important as in the professions. My famous curate who did not know the difference between a collect and a gargle is not the only man in the world whose career is wrecked & whose work is spoiled for want of the physical drill of rhetoric.

Finally, there remains for permanent endowment the municipal theatre: the chief art department of our rapidly developing Collectivism. I shall have something to say about that when the preliminary experiments I have suggested are settled; for the present it would take too much of your space & my time.

You may as well put the above into the Express as it stands: it may do something to shape the nebula.

Yrs

G. Bernard Shaw.

Neither his autobiography nor any standard biography of Andrew Carnegie (1835–1909), the Scotch-American multi-millionaire who in the last two decades of his life seemed in his incredible philanthropy to be following the doctrine preached by Shaw in *Socialism for Millionaires* (1901), records that he ever expressed any interest in endowing a permanent repertory theatre. The only reference to his own commenting on an endowed theatre that I have been able to trace is an editorial in the American *Theatre Magazine* for May, 1904, in which A. H. (Arthur Hornblow, the editor) indirectly quoted Carnegie as being strongly opposed to an endowed theatre for America and himself argued the need for one. In Carnegie's "The Gospel of Wealth" (*North American Review*, 1891, and, in book form, 1900), he enumerated seven ways that public-spirited millionaires might let the public share their wealth, but the nearest approach to building or endowing a place of entertainment was a suggestion that public halls with organs might be opened. However, on March 12, 1901, he wrote several letters announcing gifts of $4,000,000, and soon after, leaving for England, said, "I have just begun to give away money." One assumes either that in some forgotten interview he was understood to have expressed a desire to endow a repertory theatre, or his known benefactions may have fathered a wishful rumor that he so desired. At any rate, it is clear that Bright had written to ask Shaw his opinions on the project and that Shaw took the project seriously. The advice here, for all the glancing humor of the opening, is eminently sound and practical. It is typical of Shaw's fairness and objectivity that while he chose an American manager to whom he was indebted for productions of *Arms and the Man* and *The Devil's Disciple*, he chose George Alexander solely as the accepted most efficient actor-manager in London. At some time in the nineties Alexander had bought the British rights to Sudermann's *Sodom's Ende*, and had asked Shaw to translate and adapt it, but the answer was "Nothing doing," and no St. James's production was realized. . . . Where and when Alexander proposed his "scheme" I cannot discover (his biographer, A. E. W. Mason, who had played the Russian officer in the 1894 *Arms and the Man*, makes no reference to it), but what it was is clear from Shaw's description. And his mention of it leads Shaw into a "capsule" statement of his constant demand as both musical and dramatic critic for pure diction and sure projection. The "famous curate" had been suggested to Shaw's sense of humor by his attendance at a singing of the *St. John's Passion* at St. Anne's, Soho (reported in *The World*, February 18, 1891), at which he was shocked by the unintelligibility of the treatment of the whole service: ". . . I cannot help looking at a service just as I look at an opera (and I should be a very poor critic indeed if I did not take my function to be as religious a one as a man can discharge, and one which, if it is not fitted to be expressed in a church, is not fit to be expressed anywhere)," and had been pleased only by an alto choirboy. His conclusion had been: "If my recollection serves me aright, the church has some warrant beyond my word for admitting that even babes and sucklings may make better ministers than gentlemen who do not seem to know the difference between a collect and a gargle." One hopes Golding Bright remembered the passage and its critical *credo*. . . . As a dramatic critic, in his *Saturday Review* column for January 22, 1898, Shaw was to record his delight at finding clergymen who could "speak better than actors . . . in the presence of greater masters than their own personal success," actually performing in an ecclesiastical drama, *The Conversion of England*, by the Rev. Henry Cresswell, at the Great Hall of the Church House, Westminster. . . . And as dramatic critic, he had written as early as March 21, 1896, on behalf of "Municipal Theatres." . . . Note that by this time Bright had moved from *The Sun* to the London *Daily Express.*

31. Shaw Records More Disappointment concerning a Production and with the Stage Society

10, Adelphi Terrace, W.C.
6th Nov. 1901.

Dear Golding Bright

I have just received a letter from the Stage Society concerning "Mrs. Warren's Profession". It says:—"Miss Fanny Brough withdraws: she was under a misapprehension, it appears, and accepted a part in a play by you not knowing anything about the particular play."

You may take it as a safe rule that everything that is settled about the Stage Society will be unsettled next day.

Yrs
G. Bernard Shaw.

This short note is self-explanatory. The next three letters deal with the same subject, so I postpone comment.

32. On Golding Bright's Marriage and More about Mrs. Warren

8 Nov 1901.

Piccard's Cottage   10, Adelphi Terrace, W.C.
St. Catherine's
Guildford.

Dear Golding Bright

When I gave you that advice what was in my mind was that you were as likely as not to marry your landlady's daughter in a fit of sentimentality. I did not foresee that you would rush so violently to the other extreme as to marry George Egerton. How do you like it?

Mrs. Warren, if produced at all, will be produced on the 8th Dec. and repeated as usual on the 9th. Fanny Brough will play Mrs. Warren, and Miss Mackintosh Vivie: Granville Barker will probably play Frank: the rest of the cast is too conjectural to be stated yet. It is quite possible that the performance may fall through owing to difficulties about the theatre; but we must assume for the present that the play is going to be done, and treat its abandonment, if abandoned it be, as a separate piece of news for subsequent publication.

My Municipal work is certainly interfering very seriously with my dramatic activity; but I have a new play in hand for all that.

Yours sincerely
G. Bernard Shaw.

Since "that advice" does not appear in any of the preceding letters, may we assume that mentor and novice had met each other some time after November 11, 1895, and communicated in person as well as by letter? . . . "George Egerton" was the pen name of Mary Chevelita Dunne, a contributor to *The Yellow Book,* a well-known contemporary novelist of what Lennox Robinson has called a "precious" kind. (Does this imply *fin-de-siècle*-ish? And does it explain Shaw's "the other extreme"?) She was fourteen years older than Bright, and had already survived two husbands, as she was to survive Golding Bright by over four years. . . . Despite Lennox Robinson's recording that Bright came back from his honeymoon rather depressed and explained to a friend that George-Mary "always went to bed with a Russian dictionary," one assumes that whatever answer, if any, he may have given Shaw in 1901, eventually he did like it, for the marriage lasted, as opposed to the lady's earlier one-year and ten-year periods, for forty years, and by the time of Golding's death on April 14, 1941, he was known mainly as the husband of "George Egerton." Ten days after his death, a friend recorded her, in the London *Times,* as "his devoted companion during 40 years of married life, who nursed him throughout his last illness." . . . *Mrs. Warren's Profession* was again to be postponed, as Shaw anticipated. . . . The "new play in hand" was *Man and Superman,* begun in 1901, but not completed until 1903.

33. The Star Agrees to Play, but a Theatre Is Lacking

10, Adelphi Terrace, W.C.
30 Nov 1901

Dear Golding Bright
The story of Mrs Warren may as well be advanced a stage further, now that Mrs Langtry has repudiated so indignantly

the statement (which nobody made) that the performance was going to take place at the Imperial Theatre.

It is quite true that Miss Fanny Brough, on learning the nature of Mrs Warren's Profession, revoked her consent to play. But it is also true that on Miss Brough's proceeding to read the so-called wicked play, she energetically and enthusiastically withdrew her objection, resumed the part, and will, I guarantee, very considerably astonish two classes of people in it: namely, those who are now scribbling about the play without having read it, and those (mostly managers) who are under the impression that Miss Brough is only a comic actress.

The truth is, there has been a rally round the play which has astonished me. I opposed its production by the Stage Society on the ground that it might expose the manager of the theatre to the resentment of the Censor, who has unhappily committed himself to the old censorial position that illicit sexual relations must not be mentioned on the stage unless, as in the case of the Dame aux Camellias, Zaza, and Iris, the heroines of them are made extremely attractive, so as to offer the largest possible inducements to poor girls in the gallery to follow their example. As it is clear that Mrs Warren will not make a single convert to the cause of Polyandry, the King's Reader of Plays will not tolerate her; but even his department has gone so far as to disclaim any cognizance of a performance which will be open to the public for payment at the doors. Still, I urged the Society to let it alone, and suggested the substitution of my fully authorised and licensed play. The Philanderer. But the Society strongly objected to the morals and tone of The Philanderer, and overbore me as to Mrs Warren. They would have it; and the cast would have it; and, in short, I had to withdraw my prudent objections in some disgrace, which served me right.

There has been no difficulty whatever with anyone, save only the Censor and Mrs. Langtry, on the score of the play's character: quite the contrary. I had no suspicion that the play had made such an impression, although I of course knew from its reception by the reviewers on the publication of Plays, Pleasant and Unpleasant (to the horror of the then young and innocent R.G.B.), that there was danger of its being misunderstood as a mere impropriety. You will see by the letter from the National Vigilance Society in The Times today, that Mrs Warren is as busy and prosperous as ever in real life, in spite of all the committees that have been formed throughout Europe to suppress her. Alfred Place and its neighborhood is as crowded as ever with knots of women; and it is still not possible to say truthfully to one of them that she will be better treated and better paid by Society if she turns "honest" and takes to charwoman's work at the St Pancras standard of five shillings a week.

The cast is—Mrs Warren—Fanny Brough; Vivie Warren—Madge McIntosh; the Reverend Samuel Gardner—Charles Goodhart; Frank Gardner—Granville-Barker; Praed—Julius Knight; and Crofts—tell you later on, as we are changing.

You will observe that none of these people have any inducement to play except the purely artistic inducement. They won't be paid; and they are not nobodies or novices. Their names and positions, and those of the Committee of the Stage Society are sufficient cards to play against the view to which the Censor has lent his countenance.

The sole obstacle to the performance is the intimidation of the Censor, and his absolutely autocratic power—to ruin any West End manager who offends him, without reason given or remedy available. But though he cannot divest himself of his powers, he has, to do him justice, disclaimed, as far as he officially can, any concern with private performances. And the disclaimer has been made in reply to an inquiry in connection with this performance and this play. It is still probable, however, that the performance will take place out of his jurisdiction.

All of which information I recommend to your best discretion in case you should be dealing with the subject in the Daily Express or elsewhere. It must figure as your own information, because I am not justified in making any official communication to the press without consulting the others; so this must be matter come to your private knowledge.

Yrs

G. Bernard Shaw.

"Mrs. Langtry" was the placidly and statuesquely beautiful Emily Charlotte Le Breton, born on the island of Jersey, whose husband brought her to London where she immediately conquered society, was painted by Sir John Millais as "The Jersey Lily," and became the companion of the Prince of Wales, later Edward VII. She appeared at the Haymarket with the Bancrofts in a charity matinée in 1881 as Kate Hardcastle and scored such a sensation because of her beauty and her very public reputation that she was engaged for a revival of Robertson's *Ours*, and remained a distinctly inept but indubitably popular star for years in both England and America. Wilde was one of her greatest admirers; "I would rather," he is reported to have said, "have discovered Mrs. Langtry than have discovered America." As a critic Shaw noticed her but once, when she opened at the Comedy February 22, 1896, in *Gossip*, by the Americans Clyde Fitch and Leo Dietrichstein, "hardly," he declared, "the class of work I am retained to criticize." He was "heavily oppressed," but noted in passing that she tried, and failed utterly, to imitate Fanny Brough's comic force. . . . The Imperial Theatre, closed for some time, had been reopened by Mrs. Langtry on April 22nd with *A Royal Necklace*, by Pierre and Claude Berton. It was typical of the lady, always on the stage smothered in jewelry if little else, to choose a piddling play with such a title, and to seek publicity and personal profit by exploiting the furore raging late in 1901 over the attempt by the Stage Society to produce *Mrs. Warren's Profession*. . . . The attractive young wantons about whose freedom from censorship Shaw waxes ironic are, of course, the Camille of Dumas *fils*; the Zaza of Pierre Berton (one of the brothers who had written Lily's current play) and Charles Simon, in which the French actress Réjane played in the original and Mrs. Leslie Carter (like Mrs. Langtry a poor actress but a beautiful woman of unsavory reputation) in an adaptation made

by her sponsor David Belasco (1899) ; and the Iris of Pinero
(1901). The King's Reader of Plays was still G. A. Redford, who
so persistently pursued Shaw and other serious playwrights, while
casually licensing the Zazas, the Irises, and the Paula Tanquerays.
. . . Shaw playfully reminded R. G. B. that he had himself been
horrified both by reading the play and by discovering the reality
(remember the letter of the preceding December 12). . . . When
Mrs. Warren was finally produced, and republished for the Stage
Society with an "Apology" by Shaw, he twice insisted that however much the critics might misinterpret Mrs. Warren and her
play, he would guarantee its approval by the Vigilance Society and
the Salvation Army.

34. Plans for Performance of *Mrs. Warren's Profession* Completed

10 Adelphi Terrace, W.C.
6th Dec 1901.

Dear Golding Bright

Mrs Warren is postponed to next year. The cast was
complete—Charles Goodhart as Crofts & Cosmo Stuart as the
Rev. Sam Gardner—and the last difficulties surmounted, when
Miss Halston (my Strange Lady in the Man of Destiny and the
original Gloria in You Never Can Tell) fell ill. Now Miss Halston
is touring with Alexander; and as Miss McIntosh is also in the
Alexander tour she had to take up so much of Miss Halston's
work that she could not go on rehearsing Vivie Warren. So we
had to give in. Probably the postponed performance will be
early in January. It must be early, as Granville-Barker's "The
Marriage of Anne Leete" is announced for the 19th. & cannot
be postponed.

I will call the attention of the S.S. to the omission of the Express from their press list. It must be accidental—probably due to compiling the list from an old press guide dating from the pre-Express era—as we need the press to encourage actors to play for us. They get nothing but their notices.

Yrs

G. Bernard Shaw.

—————————————PRIVATE———————————

P.S. The par. in the Express was excellent. Miss Brough, before I had seen it, terrified me by telling me that it stated that she was playing because she had "the courage of her opinions". !!!!

"Next year" meant only next month. The Stage Society presented the long-delayed and much debated play in the Theatre of the New Lyric Club for two matinées January 5 and 6, 1902. Margaret Halston had played in *You Never Can Tell* at the Royalty, November 26, 1898, and in *The Man of Destiny* in a matinée at the Comedy, March 29, 1901. On May 18, 1911, she was to appear as Raina to Arnold Daly's Bluntschli at the Criterion. . . . Madge McIntosh did appear as Vivie; during his career as critic, Shaw had noted her acting in 1896 as admirably natural but unexciting. One gathers six years of experience had matured her, for an unexciting Vivie is inconceivable. . . . Charles Goodhart had appeared as the Lieutenant in a single performance of *The Man of Destiny* in March, and in May and June, 1905, he was to play Roebuck Ramsden in *Man and Superman* for fourteen performances at the Court. . . . Less than four years before this production Shaw had referred to Cosmo Stuart as "rather a heavy juvenile," scarcely the type one should expect to play the weak and hypocritical elderly Gardner. . . . Granville-Barker, whose name was later to be linked firmly with that of Shaw as director and sponsor of the Court years, had appeared in Stage Society performances as Marchbanks in July, 1900, and as Napoleon in March, 1901. . . . His play was produced by himself for the Stage Society at the Royalty January 26 and 27. . . . Fanny

Brough, whose work Shaw had always liked, but whom as early as October 1897 he had declared "an habitually underparted tragicomic actress," startled the two small audiences by essaying such a part as that of Mrs. Warren, and won from the author the gift of a photograph on the mount of which he identified himself as "The man who knows that Fanny Brough is a great actress." Shaw's good friends Grein and Archer were both horrified and indignant, but Grant Richards proudly produced a special edition of the play, with pictures of the performance taken by F. H. Evans (reproduced in Mander and Mitchenson's *Theatrical Companion*), and a new preface by Shaw called "The Author's Apology," one of his finest pieces of self-revelation and confession of dramaturgic theory. In this piece he recounted the difficulties author, actors, and sponsors had met in trying to get the play produced, difficulties not only in finding a stage for the final performance but even rehearsal-space (Allan Wade claimed in 1951, in the Shaw Memorial issue of *Drama*, that thirteen theatres, two music-halls, three hotels, and two picture galleries had refused permission), difficulties with the censor, difficulties with the journalists who attended the second performance. He particularly praised the chivalry of the Stage Society in resisting the "terror of the Censor's powers," referring to an article he had written for the *North American Review* in August, 1899, on "The Censorship of the Stage in England," wherein he had neatly summed up views already expressed and which he was to continue to express (notably before the Joint Select Committee of the House of Lords and the House of Commons on the Stage Plays in 1909), concluding with these sentences: "Desiring to give a judicial air to this article, I have racked my brains and searched my pretty exhaustive experience as a critic of the theatre to find a single item to the credit of the Censorship's account in the books of the Recording Angel. I find none." He ended the "Apology" with an expression of gratitude for the artistic spirit of the actors, especially that of Fanny Brough, who, he claimed, in the second performance "achieved the apparently impossible feat of surpassing herself," and turned most of the critics into Partridges by so convincing them that they "did not recognize [her work] as acting at all."

35. News about Translations and Productions in Austria and Germany

10 Adelphi Terrace, W.C.
23rd Feb. 1903.

Dear Golding Bright

Are you going to Vienna to see the first night of The Devil's Disciple ("Ein Teufelskerl") at the Raiemund Theatre, with Wiene as Dick Dudgeon and Thaller as Burgoyne? Of course not. Neither am I. But that first night is fixed for the day after tomorrow—Wednesday the 25th.

The Censorship has stepped in and forbidden (for the present) the production of Arms & The Man ("Helden") at the Burg Theatre, Vienna, because of the political excitement about Macedonia and Bulgaria. People who thought that the play was comic opera and not history will now, I hope, hide their diminished heads.

In Berlin there is another row over Arms & The Man. The Social-Democratic Stage Society of Berlin (the Freie Volks-bühne) want to perform the play; but Paul Lindau objects strongly on behalf of the Deutsches Theater, at which the play is to be produced in the regular way. The Social-Democrats say that they cannot be prevented from giving a "private" perform-ance of a play by a world-renowned Socialist. Lindau threatens legal proceedings. The author & the translator (Siegfried Tre-bitsch) play Spenlow & Jorkins, Shaw declaring that he prefers a Socialist audience because his plays are intended for excep-tionally intelligent people, but that Herr Trebitsch (Mr. Jorkins) must be consulted in the matter; and Trebitsch regretting that his contract with Herr Lindau makes it impossible for him to comply.

"Candida" has been secured by the Dresden Hoftheater. All this means that Trebitsch's translations of Candida, Arms & The Man, & The Devil's Disciple have made a sensation in Germany, where the English drama has hitherto been utterly despised, and that there is a Bernard Shaw boom on in the Kaiser's realm and in Austria.

I write you this as Trebitsch will be grateful if it gets into the English papers; and it occurred to me that it might help you to pad a column. It is quite fresh: I have not mentioned it to anyone else.

Yrs ever
G. Bernard Shaw.

Siegfried Trebitsch, a young Viennese journalist, had come to London on a second visit in 1900 to write letters home on the contemporary English stage and to pass his job as his father's business representative on to his successor. Seeking advice and help from William Archer, he had heard of Shaw's plays and had bought the three volumes so far published and taken them back to Austria with him. Immediately he began to try to interest theatrical agents in the German rights to Shaw's comedies, with no success. Returning to London in the fall, he paid a visit to 10 Adelphi Terrace, and, winning the assistance of Charlotte Shaw, got permission to undertake German translations. Back in Vienna, he began his self-appointed task with *The Devil's Disciple*, which he called *Ein Teufelskerl*, not intended as a direct translation of the Shavian title, but rather of a phrase used of Shaw by one of the editors of the *Neue Freie Presse*, who accepted an article by Trebitsch on "this man with the pious name," because it was interesting, although he believed the young journalist was perpetrating a hoax about "this devil of a chap." So Trebitsch, regarding Dick Dudgeon as an autobiographical portrait, changed the title to "A Devil of a Chap." Next he translated *Candida*, whose title obviously he could not change, and then *Arms and the Man*, to which he gave "the popular-sounding title," *Helden (Heroes)* since he refused to consider the literal rendering, *Waffestaten besingt mein Gesang und den Mann*. The three plays were published early in 1903 as *Drei Dramen von Bernard Shaw*. (Until 1953, the Trebitsch story had to be pieced together from newspaper and magazine articles or accepted in Archibald Henderson's version in his 1932 biography. But in that year Trebitsch produced his memoirs, translated as *Chronicle of a Life* by Eithne Williams and Ernst Kaiser. Over a quarter of this work is concerned in whole or in part with Shaw. Unfortunately the Viennese, in his eighties, had no love of precise dates and suffered from definite lapses of memory; for instance, he thinks that when he met Shaw at the beginning of the century the latter was not only still a music critic but was still known as "Corno di Bassetto," the pseudonym which Shaw had last used on May 16, 1890, when he left "Tay Pay" O'Connor and *The Star*. But the contact between playwright and translator was a long and pleasant one, and in 1922 Shaw paid Trebitsch the graceful compliment of translating *Frau Gitta's Sühne* into English as *Jitta's Atonement*. The Austrian complained that his tragedy had been turned into a comedy with a happy ending, but at least Shaw's version did receive an American production in 1923, and two short clique-ish runs in England in 1925 and 1930.) So much for the background of this letter, the first one preserved after a lapse of over a year. *Ein Teufelskerl* was produced two days later at the Raimundtheater in Vienna with Karl Wiene, whom Trebitsch had lured from the Dresden Hostheater, as Dick, and Willy Thaller, a popular comic star, as Burgoyne. Although, fifty years after the event, the Austrian translator remembered the first night as "one of the most remarkable I have ever experienced," only four performances were given. . . . Trebitsch in his rambling and rather self-satisfied autobiography does not mention the original Viennese censorial ban on *Helden,* but only the eventual successful production (he omits the date, but it was late in the 1905–1906 season) by Josef Jarno, director of the Theater in der Josefstadt, who acted Bluntschli. But this play did achieve a German production "early in 1903" (at the Berliner Theater, not the Deutsche, according to Trebitsch). . . . "Spenlow & Jorkins" are the partner-proctors in

David Copperfield to whom the hero is articled. Shaw was poking fun at his translator by identifying him as the gentle, retiring Jorkins, and himself as the Spenlow who claimed his partner's inscrutability prevented his complying with inconvenient requests. ... *Candida* was produced at the Dresden Court Theatre on November 14, 1903, by Count Seebach, with Klara Salbach and Paul Wiecke in the leading roles.

...

II. CORRESPONDENCE WITH A "YOUNG CRITIC" TURNED PLAY-AGENT

36. The "Young Critic" Has, after Ten Years, Become a Play-Agent. Mr 31, '04.

The following twelve entries are not individually very exciting, but some general introduction to them must be given here. Elisabeth Marbury (Shaw consistently spelled her first name with a *z*, but the lady, who should have the choice, equally consistently used an *s*), child of a well-to-do New York family of mixed Quaker and Huguenot stock, had been only about thirty when, in 1885, she was persuaded by Daniel Frohman, after he had observed her directing and arranging a benefit performance that netted $5,000, to become a literary agent and play-broker. Her first venture was as representative for Mrs. Frances Hodgson Burnett in the dramatization of *Little Lord Fauntleroy*. Both women made money in America, and finally Miss Marbury was persuaded by "a slick and persuasive" manager to put her savings into an Australian tour of the play, and eventually to sail for France to arrange a production there. He absconded with her investment and the Australian profits and she arrived in Paris with only $300. But her instinct for business made her seek out the most popular French dramatist, Victorien Sardou, and convince him that he and his fellow-playwrights would make more money by letting her arrange the productions of their plays in America and Great Britain on a royalty basis than they had been accustomed to receive from an outright sale of English-translation rights. She established herself by a first contact with Charles Frohman as producer and William Gillette as adapter of a very typically French farce into "a wholly innocuous entertainment." Soon she represented all the most successful French dramatists of the late nineteenth century, and began to assemble a stable of

American playwrights, starting with Clyde Fitch. Next she established a London office and with Golding Bright's older brother Arthur Addison (described at his death as "dramatic author and manager") as her representative there she began to make contacts with the English playwrights. She tried to help the broken Oscar Wilde; she acted in London for Sardou when Irving produced his *Madame Sans-Gène, Robespierre,* and *Dante;* in America she represented Shaw in dealing with the Mansfield productions of *Arms and the Man* and *The Devil's Disciple;* and long before the date of the first postcard given below Shaw had sent her amusing letters, addressed to "rapacious Elizabeth Marbury" and accusing her of turning him into a capitalist. . . . According to the lady, at the death of Addison Bright (May 29, 1906), whom she had valued as the warm friend of many English men of letters, she "had the extreme good fortune of persuading" Golding to take over his work. But Miss Marbury wrote her memoirs in 1923, when she was sixty-seven, and her memory must have been at fault, for the letter below of April 15 suggests, and that of April 30, 1904, makes clear that Golding was already working for her in the London office two years before Addison's death. . . . The point of this brief postcard probably lies in the fact that Arnold Daly, a young Irish-American actor who had become interested in the stage when he was an office-boy for Charles Frohman, in 1899 read *Plays, Pleasant and Unpleasant,* and at once conceived the idea of producing *Candida* and secured the American acting rights from Elisabeth Marbury, who had known him since his office-boy days. He was not able, however, to arrange a production until late in 1903; in less than a month after the date of this short message, on April 23, 1904, Daly was to take *Candida* on tour after a triumphant metropolitan run of over 150 nights. One gathers that, elated over his having arrived as actor and manager, Daly had asked his agent, apparently on one of her frequent visits to England, to ask Shaw for a "souvenir."

POST CARD

Post marked
London Mr 31, '04.

Miss Elizabeth Marbury
20 Green Street
Leicester Square
W.C.

Bother the souvenir! I will post a photograph to Mr. Daly on Friday: that is all I can do for him.

G. B. S.

37-38. G. B. S. and Amateur Rights

6th April 1904.

Address Telegrams
to "Socialist London"

10 Adelphi Terrace,
London W.C.

Dear Miss Wooldridge

If you receive any applications for amateur performances of my plays, the fee is £5.5.0 for one performance and £8.8.0 for two.

I shall, as soon as I can find time, get a list of the plays printed, with the terms, in such a form that you can answer enquiries by sending a copy without writing explanations.

Yours faithfully
G. Bernard Shaw.

10 Adelphi Terrace, W.C.
14th April 1904

Dear Miss Wooldridge

I am drafting a circular about the amateur rights of my plays. Have you any other authors for whom you act in this way? If so, the circular might as well include them.

By the way, I believe you could get a lot of business in this way if you were to send a prospectus (of a sort) to the Authors Society & ask to have it submitted to the dramatic committee.

❋   ❋   ❋   ❋   ❋   ❋   ❋   ❋   ❋   ❋   ❋

Yours faithfully,
G. Bernard Shaw,

Ada Wooldridge was the secretary in Elisabeth Marbury's London office for at least six and a half years longer (Shaw last wrote to her in October 1910, so far as this correspondence is concerned). In his early days, when his plays were so slowly finding production on the stage, and when amateur producing groups were not so common and therefore not so controllable as they began to be after World War I, Shaw kept a careful eye, as we shall find even more in later correspondence with those in charge at 20 Green Street, on amateur performances. . . . As late as 1910, "E. F. S." (Edward Fordham Spence), whom I have hazarded as the author of the letter Shaw mentioned on March 9, 1897, included a few snide and nasty pages on " 'G. B. S.' and the amateurs" in his *Our Stage and Its Critics*, denouncing "pretty George's way" as "a rather needless fury." . . . In his last three decades, however, Shaw, as, for instance, opposed to Barrie, was exceedingly generous in his dealings with amateurs, on the royalty question everywhere, and even in helping with production in England. . . . It is typical that

Shaw should make practical suggestions to the play agency about how to get more business.

39. The Adviser Seeks the Aid of the New Play-Agent

10, Adelphi Terrace, W.C.
15th April 1904.

Dear Golding Bright

Daly's project is utter lunacy: he would get nothing by it but a load of debt that would cripple him for the next ten years. I have written to him like a father about it; and he knows by this time that I shall not withdraw Candida.

Our business is to keep him quiet; so that he may produce You Never Can Tell next season in New York & make a solid success of it. There is not much gilding on Candida gingerbread except for the author: there is not much to be made out of £450 a week by any manager, even with the cheapest play on the stage.

Yrs ever
G. Bernard Shaw.

The following item, on an Italian postcard, addressed to Elisabeth Marbury's London office, proves that Bright was already working under his brother there. . . . In a week and a day Arnold Daly was to close his successful New York run of *Candida* and take it on tour. "Daly's project" could refer to the tour itself or to Daly's venture of playing *The Man of Destiny* as an afterpiece to the long play for three weeks. If not literally "utter lunacy," the project forced Daly a year later to admit that the double bill, keeping him on stage for three hours and twenty-five minutes, was "an evidence merely of man's overleaping ambition and pride of strength." A nervous breakdown resulted. I suspect the suggestion "to keep [Daly] quiet" supports the idea that it was the playing of both demanding parts that worried Shaw.

40. More Advice to the Play-Agent on Amateur Rights

10, Adelphi Terrace, W.C.
30th April 1904.

Dear Golding Bright

I start tomorrow to Rome for a month, dead beat.

I send you a rough draft of a circular which I began.

You must keep this list of amateur business carefully distinct from your general list. . . . Pinero writhes under the 20%, I believe; and you could get us all if you set about it seriously.

My address for the next three weeks will be 32 Via Porta Pinciana, Rome, where letters on business (unless they contain cheques) will not receive the smallest attention.

Yrs ever
G. Bernard Shaw.

41. Playwright Asks Agent's Advice

32 Via Porta Pinciana.
Rome. 13th May 1904.

Do you know anything of an American actress named Miss Grace Filkins (Mrs. Marix). She wants to play Captain Brassbound's Conversion, and says she has just the right position on the stage for it. Unfortunately I never heard of her. Have you? or has Miss Marbury?

G. Bernard Shaw.

CARTOLINA POSTALE ITALIANA

(Carte Postale d'Italie)

R. Golding Bright, Esq.
20 Green St. Leicester Square,
L'Inghilterra, Londra.   London E.C.

Whatever answer Golding Bright gave concerning the ambitious actress (and surely Miss Marbury must have heard of her), we need only report that Grace Filkins, apparently of a Philadelphia socialite family, had begun a stage career in a children's company in *Pinafore* in 1879, by 1886 had become for a time a member of Augustin Daly's company, had played many small parts in New York and on tour with Modjeska, McKee Rankin, Rosina Vokes, and Sol Smith Russell, had married Admiral Adolph Marix, U.S.N., and had appeared on tour in 1902 with Otis Skinner in a dramatization of Stevenson's *Prince Otto*. Although she continued to appear upon the stage rather sporadically and never with resounding success until her death in the mid-thirties, she apparently, neither in May, 1904, nor at any other later period, attained "just the right position on the stage" to play Lady Cicely Waynflete, and no Shavian role is listed among her many roles in a stage-career lasting nearly half a century.

42. Arnold Daly Visits Playwright and Agent

10, Adelphi Terrace, W.C.
28 June, 1904.

Dear Golding Bright

Daly is coming here at 1. Tell him that you have no instructions but that you understand that his plan of producing You Never Can Tell next winter & Mrs. Warren's Profession in the spring is quite agreeable to me and that you have no doubt that I will give him an agreement on the Candida terms if he asks me for it. Be kind to him; and when he occasionally explains (under the impression that he is the author & owner of my plays) what he will do with them, or allow or disallow to be done with them, in America, do not attempt to cure him of his delusion, as his enthusiasm will be all the keener for his believing that the works are his own. He is a likeable lad.

Thanks for Miss Rehan's address.

Yrs ever
G. Bernard Shaw.

Writing in May, 1905, for an American weekly, Arnold Daly recorded "Some Impressions of Bernard Shaw," gathered not only from working in five of the plays but from a meeting with him in the early summer of 1904 when, following the near "mental disaster as a resultant effect of overwork" from playing Marchbanks and Napoleon on his double bill, the actor visited London to "confer with Bernard Shaw as to further productions." With the kindly comments above of the wise and tolerant Dublin Irishman of forty-eight upon his second active American sponsor, it is amusing to compare the Brooklyn Irishman's picture of "an ordinary-looking man, but a bitter fighter," with "a huge contempt for the weaknesses and follies of human nature," barely recognizable Shavian characteristics to those of us who may not have met the man but feel we know him. Still Daly did find Shaw also "a genial, kindly man," who mingled "a great pity" with his contempt: "A man with a heart, a mental socialist with big ideas, who, surgeonlike, cuts away the gangrene to save the healthy life." . . . Obviously Shaw had met Daly before this note was written. I do not understand the "coming here"; why Bright should meet the American at the Shaws' apartment is not clear. (Of course, "here" might mean London, but where, then, had Shaw met him?) . . . Daly had tried to talk Shaw into collaborating with him on a play about Cromwell. Shaw neatly side-tracked him by agreeing to give him another one-acter by the fall to play with *The Man of Destiny*. Obviously, however a "likeable lad" Daly seemed, the playwright, who in any case never had worked in double-harness and was always to work alone, could not quite see him as Napoleon and Cromwell on one bill.

43-44. G.B.S. Tries to Get Ada Rehan to Play Lady Cicely

The Old House, Harmer Green,   10, Adelphi Terrace, W.C.
Welwyn, Herts.   3rd July 1904.

Dear Miss Marbury

    I have seen Miss Rehan, and read the play to her. The result is quite satisfactory: she is converted and enthusiastic. She says she is engaged by Shubert for 16 weeks. I have promised to wait as long as she likes. She wants to play both in London & America. That is all, so far. She looks fine, and will be as good as ever she was in a play by

Yrs ever
G. Bernard Shaw.

The Old House, Harmer Green,   10 Adelphi Terrace, W.C.
Welwyn, Herts.   5th July 1904.

    I should very greatly prefer a London production of Brassbound in the first instance, as I could then rehearse it myself. It is better to take a play from London to New York than bring it from N.Y. to London. If I could arrange this for next spring I should make Miss R. hold her hand this winter. Frohman is the man for it, & he could engage Drew to support him. Do nothing until you hear further from me. I am pulling the wires tentatively.

G. B. S.

The reason for the double address at the head of the two letters above as well as the next two, one gathers, is that Shaw had taken some stationery with a printed address from London to the summer home he and Charlotte had rented, so that he could work on the new play. He told Florence Farr The Old House was *his* "new house," and Ellen Terry that it was "a 16th or at latest 17th century house—a gem." The play he had read to Ada Rehan, Augustin Daly's great star, was *Captain Brassbound's Conversion*. Shaw, although like all good critics of his time he had admired the Irish-American actress's real talent, had lamented Daly's keeping her restricted to a repertory of mutilated Shakespeare and adaptations of dull German farces when the great women's parts in Ibsen were available, just as he had publicly and privately damned Irving for barring Ibsen from the Lyceum and Ellen Terry from playing Nora, Hedda Gabler, Mrs. Alving, and Ella Rentheim. Early in June, after not writing to her for a whole year, Shaw had made one last desperate plea to Ellen to play just six matinées as Lady Cicely in the fall at the Court for Barker and Vedrenne, offering to teach her the part "speech by speech." In two days she had refused because of a provincial tour already arranged, although she said she would have found the Court experience "pleasant." Not realizing that two years later, in the spring of 1906, she would play the part at the Court for over twelve weeks, Shaw decided to offer the play written especially for her to Ada Rehan. Late in July he wrote to Ellen of his reading the play to the American actress—"badly"— "I was not at my best or she would have expired with amazement." To his "dear Ellen" he enlarged upon Ada's enthusiastic conversion (I assume "converted" is a pun), reporting her as finally realizing from his reading that Lady Cicely was "a real woman." But already by July 26, he and Miss Rehan had agreed to disagree, not so much because of anything concerned with the play but because the Irishman Shaw refused to take back his critical disparagements of Augustin Daly and the Irishwoman Rehan refused equally stubbornly to forgive him for attacking her still-idolized Svengali manager star-maker. Although Ada Rehan did not die until 1916, she virtually retired from the stage in 1906. . . . The Shubert she was engaged by in 1904 was brother Sam; the Frohman of the second note was brother Charles; the man Shaw hoped for as Brassbound was Ada Rehan's former leading man with Daly's company, John Drew. . . . I assume the second note, like the first, was addressed to Miss Marbury.

45-46. Bright's Novelist Wife Turns Playwright

The Old House, Harmer Green   10, Adelphi Terrace, W.C.
20th July 1904.

It happens that this is the fifth anniversary of the foundation of the S.S., and also the day of the birth of the new Incorporated S.S. This involves a change of office & address, particulars of which have not yet reached me—stop: I do know: the address is 9 Arundel St, Strand W.C. Send the script to the secretary of the S.S. It will be a godsend to the society if it will pass Redford. My wife is on the reading committee; so I shall steal a look at it if I may.

G. B. S.

R. Golding Bright Esq.
The Gables,
Commonside East
Mitcham.

The Old House, Harmer Green,   10, Adelphi Terrace, W.C.
Welwyn, 28th July 1904.

The Stage Society is compiling a list of "the following plays are under consideration" for its prospectus of next season. A play by George Egerton would add to the decoration considerably; but nothing of the sort has arrived yet. Has the distinguished author changed her mind?

Tell Lorraine that in consequence of the distressingly high standard of sanity among managers, the demand for Man & Superman is deplorably slack. Even Daly has not mentioned it.

G. B. S.

R. Golding Bright Esq.
Miss Elizabeth Marbury
20 Green St
Leicester Square
W.C.

The first performance sponsored by the Stage Society, November 26, 1899, had been Shaw's own *You Never Can Tell*. One assumes the first meeting to enlist subscribers, held in Frederick Whelen's rooms, occurred on July 20. When the Society was incorporated, Shaw was elected a member of the Council of Management, and served on the casting and production committee for years. . . . Apparently George Egerton changed her mind about submitting a script for fall production by the Society, for her first recorded play is *His Wife's Fancy*, 1908. In 1910, a second play, *The Backsliders*, failed in an American production, starring the charming Annie Russell, because, according to George C. Tyler, guiding spirit of the producing firm of Liebler and Co., "it was just too brilliant for public consumption." I can find no recorded performance of her third play, *Camilla States Her Case*, 1925. . . . In the second note Shaw mentions for the first time in this correspondence Robert Loraine, a young English actor who had scored in romantic roles in America after the turn of the century and who was to become one of the most famous stars associated mainly with Shavian parts. . . . *Man and Superman* had been published in 1903. Loraine, who had been a Shaw-worshipper ever since as a critic the older man had managed an encouraging phrase or even sentence for the young actor's first minor performances, got a copy early, and read it on a train while touring in America, and immediately fell in love with the part of John Tanner. But he could not interest in Shaw's play even those American managers who were eager to star

him because they found the play difficult to understand, so Loraine
cabled to London for the purchase of performing rights. . . . Shaw
claimed, in one of several passages which he added to the biography
of the actor written by his wife Winifred, that he originally held
up negotiations (as of the end of July, 1904, obviously) because
he still thought of Loraine as the young juvenile he had found
promising toward the end of his career as dramatic critic and
found it difficult to think of him as an actor-manager, the status
to which the young man was, with no assets, promoting himself.

47-50. Mansfield Replaced as American Shavian Producer by Daly and Loraine

---

10 Adelphi Terrace, W.C.
27th October 1904.

Dear Miss Wooldridge

Miss Marbury is now negotiating with Loraine & cabling
direct to me; so you may leave the matter in my hands.

yours faithfully
G. Bernard Shaw.

Miss Elizabeth Marbury,
20 Green St
Leicester Square
W.C.

Address telegrams   27th October 1904.   10 Adelphi Terrace
to "Socialist London"   London, W.C.

Dear Golding Bright

I cabled direct to Miss Marbury last night to say that I
would not take 700 dollars a week for Man & Superman from

Mansfield, but that I would take 960 dollars or 120 dollars a performance. I was screwed up to this pitch of avarice by a glance at the returns in 1898 from the Devil's Disciple, which made seven hundred dollars seem paltry. Further I said that I preferred my 10%. I also signified that she ought to try Loraine, if only to put a stop to his idiotic cabling to Green St with Miss Marbury within five minutes walk. What the devil does he mean by it?

You may tell all and sundry that Candida is not in the market for this winter. I have resolved to keep it until it has been worked up a bit more in London.

Tell Miss Marbury that the Irish play is a peculiar product, and might possibly lead to lynching if exploded on an excitable Irish population in a lawless country like America. I promised to let Daly have it if You Never Can Tell fails and leaves him stranded. I read a bit of it to him, and was struck by the way in which he caught hold of it.

Daly, by the way, has gone out of management on his own account, and has signed himself into slavery to Liebler & Co for five years. He says he is to have "supreme charge back of the stage as regards the selection of the plays, players &c." This may be good news and it may be bad. Ask Miss Marbury which.

I am much applied to from America just now to lecture. Both Daly and Shubert have this idea. I never like to say no: so tell Miss Marbury to say, if they ask her, that I am a very good lecturer, and that my terms are a million dollars for a tour, not including the salary of Paderewski at the piano.

In short, you had better send this letter on to your principal, with my homages.

Yours faithfully
G. Bernard Shaw.

10 Adelphi Terrace, W.C.
16th Nov. 1904.

Dear Golding Bright

  I promised to take 5% for what we should call No 3 towns—for places to which it was clearly not worth Daly's while to go. But of course this does not mean that he can send a company to Chicago & pay me 5% merely because he is not playing himself. I should not of course object to his banging in a stray No 2 town to sweeten the bargain for the poor wretch to whom he sublets his refuse; but I should demur to any town of, say, more than 100,000 population going in that way.

  In short, I will take 5% in places where the piece evidently would not be produced at all at the higher percentages.

Yrs ever
G. Bernard Shaw.

10, Adelphi Terrace, W.C.
22nd Nov. 1904.

  I will fix up a meeting with Tyler this week if I can extricate myself for a moment from rehearsals.

  There will be a bit of fight on the S.S. committee over the plays to be produced this season. With two such trump cards as a new act, and Miss Ashwell, I shall have a try for second place (Tolstoy, whom Redford has licensed, has the first). Can you promise her? I am curious to see the new act; but that is only a matter of my personal literary appetite.

G. Bernard Shaw

R. Golding Bright Esq.
20 Green St
    Leicester Square W.C.

Not realizing Shaw's reluctance to rent rights to a youth unknown as a manager, Loraine thought he was being outbid by the now great star, Mansfield. Actually Shaw was displeased with the American's conceit over the fame and fortune which *Arms and the Man* had started and *The Devil's Disciple* made firm and fast, and with his cavalier dropping of *Candida* after a bare rehearsal trial, and with his refusal to take the American rights to *Caesar and Cleopatra*. On receiving this last refusal, Shaw had sent one of the first of his famous terse cables to Mansfield: "Farewell Pompey." . . . The note to the London secretary is explained by the end of the first paragraph in the letter of the same date to Bright—the impulsive Loraine, always improvident, was wasting his money cabling from New York to the London agency of America's best-known play-agent. . . . Obviously during the summer Mansfield had begun bidding to play John Tanner; obviously he refused Shaw's ultimatum on terms, and the farewell to Pompey remained final. . . . Loraine recorded that he was finally offered American rights only (he had hoped for the English rights as well) for £200 down in advance of the 10% of gross receipts which Shaw had "preferred" to his counter-guaranteed weekly payment from Mansfield. To finish the account of the *Man and Superman* negotiations: since £200 represented almost all his savings, Loraine sold all his possessions, even his library, to buy clothes to impress England and to book passage. Luckily he found Charles Frohman in London, on his arrival in May, 1905, eager and willing, because of the interest in the production of the play (minus *Don Juan in Hell*) at the Court the same month, to buy the American rights himself and to accept Loraine as star, and to give him "complete control of the production, casting and staging, in fact everything behind the curtain, and also to approve the theatre." After meeting Shaw, receiving full cooperation, and establishing a warm friendship which was to last until Loraine's death, the actor returned to America and opened the play at the Hudson Theatre, New York, September 5, 1905, for a nine months' run, followed by a seven months' tour. Later, beginning June 4, 1907, he gave eight matinées at the Court in London of the first production of *Don Juan in Hell*. . . . It is easy to understand Shaw's decision announced in the first letter to Bright concerning *Candida*. Daly had enjoyed spectacular success with it in America, but it was to be years before the play really became popular in England. . . . The "Irish play" was *John Bull's Other Island*, completed during the summer and to be presented at the Court for six matinées in November, 1904, and revived there for a total of over ten weeks in 1905, and six weeks in 1906. Shaw had written Ellen Terry early in September that he had finished "a big play and a little one." When Daly had visited him in the summer, he had agreed to write, as a curtain-raiser for *The Man of Destiny, How He Lied to Her Husband*, a "comedietta" satirizing the American "Candidamaniacs." Daly, on his return to America, signed a contract with the theatrical firm of Liebler and Co. for five years. In the fall he opened in New York with two bills, *Candida* and the two one-acts, and toured across country as far as San Francisco. One assumes his contract with Liebler and Co., which sounds so much like Loraine's with Frohman, was eventually accepted by both Miss Marbury and Shaw as "good news." . . . Shaw, of course, was consistently to refuse to lecture in America or really to visit there, except for a one-night visit with Hearst in California and a lecture to the American Academy of Political Science in New York (from shipboard to the Metropolitan and back to the harbor). His suggestion to Miss Marbury as to terms, if not one of his best jokes, at least gives an idea how strongly he fought, for whatever reasons, against a real visit to the United States. . . . The content of the November 16th note is explained by Daly's allowing two other companies, one starting in the late fall, the other in the spring of 1905, to tour *Candida*. . . . George C. Tyler, who described himself in his ghost-written autobiography as "a Natural Born Gambler," had risen from newspaper work through advance-work for touring companies through somewhat shady promotion work to become, late in the nineteenth century, the producing firm of Liebler and Co. (Tyler never even mentions a Christian name or initials for Liebler, who to him represented only a man with $3,000 to invest, a sum which the gambler turned into a fortune.) One assumes that the meeting between Shaw and Tyler took place, and that negotiations begun by Daly during the summer for the American rights to *You Never Can Tell* were concluded, for the play opened at the Garrick Theatre, New York, January 9, 1905, and Daly scored still another success for and with

Shaw. In 1905 Shaw tried to get Tyler to star Eleanor Robson in America in *Major Barbara.* . . . On October 12, 1914, Tyler (or Liebler and Co.) presented Mrs. Pat Campbell and Philip Merivale in *Pygmalion* at the Park Theatre, New York, and the play toured the States straight through 1915. . . . The second paragraph of the November 22nd note returns, fairly clearly, to the question of a play by Mrs. Golding Bright. Apparently the project had not been dropped or it had been revived. She seems to have written a new act and either she or her husband to have talked to Lena Ashwell, an actress of whom Shaw approved, about appearing in her play. But neither a play by George Egerton nor a part taken by Lena Ashwell appears in any of the Stage Society programs for the 1904–1905 season. It was a strong one. If Tolstoy's *The Power of Darkness* (December) did achieve "first place" (I take it Shaw referred to importance, not chronology), I suspect *Man and Superman,* sponsored for three performances by the Society before its Court run, surely deserved second. The season included plays by Gorki, Brieux (two), Yeats, and Conrad, and the first production of a famous one-act, *'Op 'o Me Thumb,* presented on the same bill with Browning's *A Soul's Tragedy.*

51-64. Strictly Business

10 Adelphi Terrace W.C.
1st Dec. 1904.

Dear Miss Wooldridge

The difficulty about the Paris performance was altogether the fault of the amateur entrepreneur, who would not explain who he was nor what he wanted. However, a friend of his and mine cleared it up. It was an ordinary amateur business

—a matter of five guineas & a stipulation that the press was not to be invited.

Yrs Faithfully
G. Bernard Shaw.

Miss Elizabeth Marbury,
20 Green St
Leicester Square W.C.

10 Adelphi Terrace W.C.
1st Dec. 1904.

Dear Miss Wooldridge

Your letter contained the a/c but not the cheque.

By the way, it may be as well to cross my cheques "London & County, Oxford St": that will make them quite safe.

Yrs faithfully
G. Bernard Shaw.

---

10 Adelphi Terrace, W.C.

Welwyn—12/12/04.

Dear Miss Wooldridge

Will you be so kind as to complete the address of the enclosed letter & post it for

Yrs faithfully
G. Bernard Shaw.

---

10 Adelphi Terrace, W.C.
25th Jan. 1905.

Please attend to this lady. £5-5-0 as usual.

G. Bernard Shaw.

---

10 Adelphi Terrace, W.C.
11th February, 1905.

Ask your American office whether they are correct in their remittances of my royalties. They seem to be calculating them at 10% for what are, as far as I can make out, one-night stands by the No 2 company.

Does Daly pay 10% on these or 5? I have not time to go into the matter accurately; and as the mistake (if any) is in my favor, I am quite content to leave it as it is.

In haste
G. Bernard Shaw.

Miss Elizabeth Marbury,
20 Green St, Leicester Sq.
W.C.

_____

10, Adelphi Terrace, W.C.

The Old House, Harmer Green,
Welwyn. 5th March, 1905.

Out of town, thank heaven! Dont mention the word production to me: I seem doomed to waste the few remaining years of my life in negotiating productions. Tell them to go away.

Is Sam Shubert over here; and if so, where?

G. Bernard Shaw.

R. Golding Bright Esq,
20 Green St, Leicester Sq.
W.C.

_____

The Old House, Harmer Green,   10, Adelphi Terrace, W.C.
Welwyn. 8th March, 1905.

I cannot take John Bull out of Daly's hands and toss it to a stranger without a word of warning. Daly has done very

well with my plays: why should I now wantonly throw him
over & let the other fellows profit by his risk & his devotion?
Tell your man to go away & write a play for himself if he wants
one.

I proposed to Tree to give a matinée for Viola of the first
act of Caesar: that is how he came to have the book &c.

I do most certainly resent being bothered about productions.
These idiots leave me in peace for ten years and then rush for
me because the King orders a performance at the Court Theatre. They will make just as great a mess of producing me as
they did before of <u>not</u> producing me. Put them out. Order
them off. Call the police, if necessary. Daly and Vedrenne-
Barker can still have me at 10%: all others 25%.

G. B. S.

R. Golding Bright Esq.
Miss Elizabeth Marbury,
20 Green St, Leicester Sq,
W.C.

---

10 Adelphi Terrace, W.C.
9/3/05. [March 9]

I will call on Shubert tomorrow at the Carlton at 5.
Was it Charles Frohman or Daniel who wanted John Bull?
Better send these people to me: I can generally arrange
something with them, if not the exact thing they fancy they
want.

G. B. S.

R. Golding Bright Esq.
Miss Marbury's
20 Green Street, Leicester Sq.
W.C

The Old House, Harmer Green,   10 Adelphi Terrace, W.C.
Welwyn. 13th March 1905.

I had to write to Frohman direct, as your revelation came the very day I had to ask him to lend me Ainley for Man & Superman. However, he lent him and was very handsome about that & things in general. You might let me know when he returns to London. I had a satisfactory interview with Sam Shubert. Probably we shall pull off Brassbound after all with Miss Rehan.

I will send you the script you ask for presently. I want to take a final look through it so as to be able to say definitely what it wants in the way of trimming.

G. B. S.

R. Golding Bright, Esq.
Miss Marbury's
20 Green St, Leicester Sq. W.C.

The Old House, Harmer Green,   10 Adelphi Terrace, W.C.
Welwyn. 22 March 1905.

DONT. I solemnly declare I will put a notice in the Era that my plays are not available for commercial theatres. Fortunately the M. of D. is too long.

G. B. S.

Rigg's Hotel, 2nd May, 1905.
Windermere.

Remittance received. Will send you proper receipt when I get back to London. Thanks.

G. Bernard Shaw.

R. Golding Bright Esq.
c/o Miss Elizabeth Marbury
20 Green St., Leicester Sq.
W.C.

c/o Colonel Cholmondeley
Edstaston, Wem, Shropshire.
(until the 13th)
11th Oct. 1905.

Dear Miss Wooldridge

Will you please cross my drafts
LONDON & COUNTY, OXFORD ST.
These uncrossed drafts-on-demand can be cashed too easily
if they go astray.

Yrs faithfully,
G. Bernard Shaw.

---

10 Adelphi Terrace, W.C.
21st Nov. 1905.

Dear Miss Wooldridge

It is really tempting Providence to send my cheques
uncrossed. The last two have come quite open—payable to anybody who writes my name on the back.
Cross them London & County, Oxford St.

Yrs ever
G. Bernard Shaw.

---

10 Adelphi Terrace, W.C.
5/12/05.

Dear Miss Wooldridge

This time you have crossed the cheques "Capital &
County." It should be London & County, Oxford St.

Yrs faithfully,
G. Bernard Shaw.

The previous eight items suggest merely the minor annoyances and troubles even of the playwright who has an agent. They are self-explanatory as to point, and unexplainable in the main as to detail. ... Of the material in the brief note to Bright dated March 8, 1905, three brief comments might be in order: 1. Daly produced *John Bull's Other Island* at the Garrick Theatre, New York, October 10, 1905; 2. The only explanation I can offer concerning the remark about Tree and his daughter is that the following month, from April 24th through the 29th, the actor-manager produced at His Majesty's his first Shakespearean Festival, presenting in one week *Richard II* (twice), *The Merry Wives of Windsor, Twelfth Night, Hamlet, Much Ado about Nothing,* and *Julius Caesar* (twice), and that Shaw, as a generous noting of Viola Tree's twenty-first year and also as an opportunity to offer some public contrast of his portrait of Caesar with Shakespeare's, may have suggested the matinée to fit somewhere in the program of that crowded week; 3. Edward VII had commanded an evening performance of Shaw's Irish play at the Court for March 11th. ... At this performance, incidentally, he, who as Prince of Wales, had thought the writer of *Arms and the Man* "must be mad," was so delighted that he broke a chair in the Royal Box while laughing at Broadbent. The Command Performance had obviously started a Shaw boom on the American dramatic market—notice the references to Sam Shubert and Charles Frohman in the notes of March 9th and 15th. ... The significance of the reference to Henry Ainley escapes me; this fine actor did not demonstrate his magnificent vocal powers in the approaching production of *Man and Superman* at the Court (May-June), and to my knowledge, appeared in only one Shavian role, that of Bishop Bridgenorth in *Getting Married* in the Vedrenne-Barker production at the Haymarket, May-June, 1908.

65-68. *Mrs. Warren's Profession* and a Frenchman's Mistake

10 Adelphi Terrace, W.C.
5th December, 1905.

It is impossible for me to accept the proposal contained in your letter dated the 20th Nov., which appears to be based on a mistaken impression of "Mrs. Warren's Profession." No doubt you have been deceived by the action of the New York Police.

The play is already translated, though the translation has not yet been published.

G. Bernard Shaw.

POST CARD
UNIVERSAL POSTAL UNION

Post mark
London Dec. 5 1905.

M. Marcel Boulestin
177BIS Rue de Courcelles
Paris.

---

10 Adelphi Terrace, W.C.
5th Dec. 1905.

My postcard to Boulestin was my answer to his application. What more does he want?

G. B. S.

R. Golding Bright Esq.
Miss Marbury's
20 Green Street, Leicester Sq.
W.C.

10 Adelphi Terrace, W.C.
28th Dec. 1905.

Can you tell me whether Mr. Charles Frohman is in London just now, &, if so, is he at the Savoy Hotel?

G. Bernard Shaw

Miss Elizabeth Marbury,
20 Green St, Leicester Sq.
W.C.

10 Adelphi Terrace, W.C.
30th January 1906.

Dear Miss Wooldridge

I notice that Mr. Arnold Daly has paid royalties on only one performance of "Mrs. Warren's Profession." There were two: one at New Haven & the famous one in New York.

I do not propose to ask Mr. Daly to pay on New Haven; but Miss Marbury may as well know of the omission.

Yrs faithfully
G. Bernard Shaw.

Arnold Daly's production of *John Bull's Other Island* failed with audience and critics in New York; the topical allusions which made it popular in London missed fire completely; he withdrew it on October 21 (1905), and, despite Shaw's advising that such a move was premature and ill-timed, put *Mrs. Warren's Profession*

into rehearsal and presented it on October 27th at the Hyperion Theatre, New Haven, Connecticut. An immediate outcry resulted in the revoking of the theatre's license. Daly took the company to New York, and on October 30th he opened the play at the Garrick. The performance was a *succès de scandale*; hundreds were turned away; ticket-scalpers made incredible profits; many attended hoping for an open display of indecency. The resultant uproar was even louder and more unintelligent than that in New Haven; the few protesting and protecting voices were drowned in the tumult of insult and invective of the mob. Daly announced he would withdraw the play, but he, the rest of the cast, and his manager were arrested on a charge of disorderly conduct and released only on payment of bail. The case dragged on in the Court of Special Sessions until July 6, 1906, when Daly and his manager were acquitted, the presiding judge's opinion admitting "the reforming influence of the play" but questioning "the method of the attack." . . . Whoever M. Marcel Boulestin may have been, his proposal obviously suggested to Shaw that he mainly hoped to cash in on the unsavory reputation the play had earned through the action of the American police after both performances. . . . Shaw had chosen as his French translator Augustin Hamon; most critics have felt the choice unwise; whether it was the fault of the translations or the inevitable result of Gallic temperament and taste, Shaw's plays were not accepted in France with anything of the reception accorded them in the German-speaking countries as translated by Trebitsch, who chose himself. . . . One assumes Shaw and Frohman were probably still discussing Loraine's American production of *Man and Superman.*

69-70. Playwright Advises Play-Agent on Business Procedure

10, Adelphi Terrace, W.C.
23rd February, 1906.

Dear Golding Bright

What authors do you collect amateur fees for besides myself? . . .

If your amateur business is at all large, or if it is worth your while to develop it, you should send a circular at least once a year to all the amateur dramatic clubs giving your list of authors & plays, terms &c &c. If it is not worth your while to do this I will send a circular on my own a/c; and I may as well include in it any other authors you are acting for.

Yrs ever
G. Bernard Shaw.

Following is a complete list of Mr. Shaw's plays up to date; but only Nos. 4, 5, 6, 7, 10 & 11 are suitable for amateurs of ordinary aims and resources. Other lists should be given of course.

Plays, Pleasant & Unpleasant

1. Widowers' Houses
2. The Philanderer
3. Mrs. Warren's Profession
} Unpleasant Plays

4. Arms & The Man
5. Candida
6. The Man of Destiny
7. You Never Can Tell
} Pleasant Plays

Three Plays for Puritans

8. The Devil's Disciple
9. Caesar & Cleopatra
10. Captain Brassbound's Conversion

11. The Admirable Bashville—
    Elizabethan parody.
12. Man & Superman.

Amateurs desirous of performing plays by the above authors should apply to Miss Elizabeth Marbury, 20 Green St., Leicester Square, London W.C. (Registered Telegraphic Address "Amarantes London"). The fee for single performances is £5.5.0. (or whatever it may be). For two performances £8.8.0. Permission must be obtained beforehand, as certain plays by these authors are not always available for amateurs.

Applications are occasionally made for the remission of fees on the ground that the performance is for the benefit of a charity. Miss Marbury begs to point out that practically all amateur performances are for the benefit of charities; so that an author who remitted fees on that ground would be not only giving a considerable part of his income in charity in addition to his direct personal contributions, but allowing amateur actors to choose the objects of his benevolence for him; and this, too, without any guarantee that the business arrangement of the performance would be economical enough to leave any surplus for the charities. Such a request is obviously unreasonable. In no case can Miss Marbury remit the fees, or forward to the author any application for their remission.

All plays in Miss Marbury's hands are fully protected, and

may not be performed without the author's authority in the United Kingdom.

Copies of Mr. Bernard Shaw's plays, at one and sixpence each, can be obtained from Miss Marbury. These are exact reprints of the original editions. The stage directions, though they contain no technical terms and seem to be of a purely literary character, contain all the information needed by the stage manager.

10, Adelphi Terrace, W.C.
10th May 1906.

Where is Miss Marbury? I had hoped to see her in Paris; but I have had to return without fulfilling any of my good resolutions, as my time was completely taken up by Rodin. Also, my letters were not forwarded: hence my delay in acknowledging the cheques.

G. B. S.

As in earlier years Shaw had written his own "copy" and interviewed himself for the journalist-protégé, so now, with equally knowledgeable business acumen, he himself prepared a brochure to attract and to direct amateur patronage for the play-bureau. . . . Of the plays listed, *The Admirable Bashville* only is here mentioned for the first time. . . . *Cashel Byron's Profession*, the fourth of Shaw's novels to be written, but the first to be published, had proved a popular success, especially in America, and, since the copyright laws at the time permitted it, had been dramatized there for a production at the Herald Square Theatre on December 17, 1900, by a Harrison J. Wolfe, who played Cashel. Shaw prepared a dramatic adaptation himself in 1901, called *The Admirable Bash-*

ville, to protect his English copyright, and a copyright performance was given at the Bijou Theatre, Bayswater, but as no program was printed, no details of cast (the license was dated 4.3.1901) can be given. Shaw never took the piece seriously, and largely as a result of this attitude, it is a pure and very joyous *jeu d'esprit*; claiming that he was pressed for time but that it is obviously easier to write passable blank verse than decent prose, Shaw produced a farcical parody, both of Elizabethan high-falutinism and of the novel itself, that is largely a fascinating pastiche of famous lines from Marlowe and Shakespeare and a very lively bit of fast and furious slapstick, made all the funnier by the impressive roll of the more than competent verse and the reminiscent incongruities of its Elizabethan echoes. . . . One has a distinct suspicion that, if this "copy" was actually adopted by Miss Marbury's London agency and if a trained Shavian were to come upon a separately preserved copy (that is, one not, like this, practically signed), he would recognize immediately the style of the longish paragraph on benefit-performances. . . . With reference to the item of May 10, 1906, we might note that Rodin made during the Paris visit a bronze bust of Shaw, much approved by the subject. In 1945 Shaw gave the bust to the Royal Academy of Dramatic Art.

71-72. Pirating in Hungary

10, Adelphi Terrace, W.C.
11th May 1906.

My plays have been purchased largely in Hungary by the theatres from various agents; and the Devil's Disciple has been produced with great success.

The Authors' Society is now taking proceedings on my behalf, as the agents omitted to mention the matter to me or to send me any of the advances they collected in my name.

In short, the answer to your question as to how the plays stand in Hungary is—STOLEN.

G. B. S.

R. Golding Bright Esq.
20 Green St, Leicester Sq.
W.C.

10, Adelphi Terrace, W.C.

The Flag of Boodle Pest.

You cannot persuade me.
If he paid hundreds he owed millions.

G. B. S.

R. Golding Bright Esq.
Miss Marbury's
20 Green St. Leicester Sq. W.C.

Archibald Henderson, like all Shaw biographers to date unfamiliar with this collection of letters, in 1932 reported a Budapest production of *The Devil's Disciple* "without popular success" on March

28, 1906, at the Comedy Theatre. This is obviously the production referred to here, but Shaw's notion of "great success" and "millions" owed by the agents fighting under "The Flag of Boodle Pest" does not indicate exact knowledge, since the whole matter to him at the time seems to have been one of rumor.

73. Inquiry after an Absent Loraine

Harmer Green, Welwyn.   10, Adelphi Terrace, W.C.
10th June 1906.

Dear Miss Wooldridge

If Mr. Robert Loraine pays you a visit, will you kindly hint to him that it would help matters if he mentioned his address in his telegraphic correspondence. I answered a wire of his to the Savoy Hotel (where he stayed when he was here last) several days ago, but have not heard from him.

> Yrs faithfully
> G. Bernard Shaw.

One can only wonder why Shaw was expecting Loraine in London. Winifred, the actor's wife, records that *Man and Superman* closed its New York run, begun on the previous September 4th, on May 28, 1906, and that it reopened on tour in September, but she makes no mention how Loraine spent his summer. She does, however, carefully note his return to London in May, 1907 to play Tanner with the Court company for five weeks, with eight matinées, beginning the third week, of *Don Juan in Hell*. During that summer (1907) Loraine was with the Shaws at Mevagissey and in the summer of 1908 he was with them again, at LLanbedr in Wales, for a week or two.

The Editor Intrudes. A Brief but Necessary Pause.

We have noted that Golding Bright had been associated with Elisabeth Marbury's London office at 20 Green Street, Leicester Square, W.C., at least since April, 1904. His older brother, Arthur Addison, an author's agent "with a spark of genius himself," who had been friend and adviser as well as business executor since 1891 to James M. Barrie, who had introduced the Scot and the actress Mary Ansell whom he married, who had first got the idea of dramatizing *The Little Minister*, and goaded Barrie into the eminently successful play-version by making one himself first, had become closely associated with Miss Marbury by 1896 and become her London representative. He had worked as a reporter on *The Sun* before Golding took over his work, and the younger brother obviously followed him also into the agency business. In 1906 it was suddenly discovered that, for no ascertainable reason—he was under no financial or other pressure—he had been for some time badly falsifying the accounts of several of his major clients; the money he had stolen he had not spent—it was intact in his own bank account; Barrie was so personally devoted to him that he wished to let Addison pay back what he had taken, but the others who had been defrauded insisted upon prosecuting. Addison suffered a general breakdown, escaped to the Continent, and on May 29 committed suicide at Lucerne. Barrie and Golding went to Switzerland to identify the body and to bring it home. It is certainly more than possible that Shaw's tact and a possible embarrassment at the unwitting and quite unintentional playing-up of the "STOLEN" motif about the Budapest piracy in the month of Addison's suicide accounts more than anything else for the gap in the correspondence at this point of over six months. Golding took over Elisabeth Marbury's London office immediately upon his brother's death.

74-106. Golding Bright as Chief of Staff

Adress telegrams to   10, Adelphi Terrace,
"Socialist London"   London W.C.
                                                         January 10th 1907.

Dear Golding Bright,

The question of "John Bull's Other Island" and the subsequent plays is settled for amateurs for the present by the
fact that none of them are as yet printed. When I have got
them through the press there is no reason why "John Bull" and
"Man and Superman" at least should not be played by amateurs if they want to. "Major Barbara" is beyond them: you are
not likely to have any applications. "The Doctor's Dilemma"
will not be printed for some time yet.

French used to reduce the 5 guinea fee to 4 guineas when
two performances were given; but on the whole I think I shall
leave matters as they are. I have no sympathy at all with amateurs on the money question, because any money they make
they give to some hospital or other, and thereby encourage the
private charity system which I have been preaching against all
my life. The money goes first into the pocket of the ratepayer,
who is relieved from the duty of providing public hospitals,
and it is then screwed out of him by the landlord as rent, the
upshot of the whole transaction being that I lose two guineas
and you lose your commission on it for the sake of the Duke
of Westminster or the Duke of Bedford.

I am greatly flattered by Leslie Stuart's desire to collaborate
with me on a musical play. Ever since 1894, I have been overwhelmed with commissions of that sort, beginning with D'Oyly
Carte, who gave me <u>carte blanche</u> for a Savoy opera and told

me I need not have Sullivan unless I chose. Then came George Edwardes, who selected me as the original librettist of the "Duchess of Dantzic". Lowenstein and others followed but that great libretto is still unwritten. Tell Stuart that I am rather keen on the idea, but that what I want to write is the music and not the libretto.

Yours ever,
G. Bernard Shaw.

---

10 Adelphi Terrace, W.C.
14/2/07.

R. Golding Bright, Esq.,
20, Green Street,
Leicester Square, W.C.

With Bernard Shaw's compliments.

By the way, 5 nights at Liverpool of You Never Can Tell is past a joke. If amateurs are going into business like this, they must pay business rates. We must confine amateurs to two performances at the outside; for this affair amounts to a breach of my understanding with Vedrenne & Barker.

G. B. S.

[The note below was typed on Miss Marbury's official letterhead, listing R. Golding Bright as "London Representative."]

London. Feb: 15th, 07.

G. Bernard Shaw Esq,
10, Adelphi Terrace,
Strand, W.C.

Dear Mr. Shaw,

In a cable just received from Australia we are asked to secure the Australian rights of "Mrs. Warren's Profession", would you let me know if you will agree to negotiate for these rights and if so what would your lowest terms be, as we have to cable the reply as soon as possible.

With kindest regards,

Yours sincerely,

Ada Wooldridge.

15/2/07.   10, Adelphi Terrace, W.C.

Certainly not at present. It will not do to begin Australian operations with Mrs. Warren's Profession. I prefer always to hold back that play until my position is firmly established with less controvertible pieces.

G. B. S.

---

10 Adelphi Terrace, W.C.

Ayot St Lawrence, Welwyn, Herts.
Station: Wheathampstead, G.N.R. 2¼ Miles.
Telegrams: Bernard Shaw, Codicote.
27th Feb. 1907.

Dear Miss Wooldridge

Seven performances mean simply seizing the Dublin rights under cover of amateurism. If the Players Club choose to give seven private performances to their own members, they can have that luxury of paying for it; but seven public performances are quite out of the question; and even to the private ones the press must not be invited.

Have we any particulars of where the performances are to take place, where the money is to go &c &c?

The Liverpool affair was bad enough; but this would be an outrageous abuse of the right to license amateurs.

I return to town tomorrow.

In haste to catch the post

Yrs

G. Bernard Shaw.

10, Adelphi Terrace, W.C.
3rd March 1907.

Dear Golding Bright

We must shut down on these Dublin people firmly. Write to them and ask them how they can possibly require the Gaiety Theatre in Dublin for a week if their performances are really amateur ones. Point out that you have no authority to deal with my plays in England except for amateur purposes, and that in any case they can hardly suppose that my plays can be performed by anyone who chooses to pay five guineas a night, at a regular theatre under commercial conditions. Say that if a club of amateurs choose to give seven performances at an occasional or private theatre for the amusement of their guests and themselves that is their own affair, and they can get permission by paying for it; but to take the second theatre in Dublin for a Shaw week, and present a play which has not been judged in that city by a professional performance, and claim amateur terms, is absurd.

If they choose to give their seven performances privately, without inviting the press, or selling tickets to the public for their own profit, or indeed selling to the public at all, then we might reluctantly permit it, as you overlooked the number seven in consenting. But if they mean business, they must make a business proposition, though there is no likelihood of their being allowed to anticipate Vedrenne & Barker.

They have done The Man of Destiny quite often enough. I shall not consent to their Shaw week, which is really a most impudent abuse of amateur business. The Liverpool affair was the last straw: I could have been sued for it if the aggrieved parties were any other than V & B; and they are not particularly pleased, naturally.

After this, you must make a cast iron rule never to permit more than two performances at the outside, and then only under genuine amateur conditions. You should be very chary indeed of giving permission for Arms & The Man, You Never

Can Tell, & the "pleasant plays" generally in No. 1 towns where they have not been seen at the regular theatres. Otherwise they may get me into no end of trouble.

Yrs faithfully
G. Bernard Shaw.

———————————

10, Adelphi Terrace, W.C.
6th March 1907.

Dear Golding Bright

Will you please read the enclosed letter from me to Ashley; make a copy of it to keep by you; and post it today.

I enclose also Ashley's letter.

What has happened is that they made money out of the Man of Destiny, and now want to make more out of Arms & The Man. It is an awkward business; and in future we must use a form of consent printed in strict terms. I shall not absolutely forbid the performances; but they must pay 10% on the gross.

Do not take any further action yourself until I have Ashley's reply.

Yours faithfully
G. Bernard Shaw.

Innisfallen, Frankfort Avenue,
Rathger, Dublin
5th March, 1907

Irish Players' Club.

Dear Sir,

I have to acknowledge receipt of your letter of the 4th inst. When we wrote you some time ago for permission to perform "The Man of Destiny" you referred us to your agent, Miss Elizabeth Marbury, from whom, you said we would get all information. Accordingly, when we desired permission to play

"Arms and the Man" we wrote this Agent (whom we presume is invested with full powers regarding such matters) asking for permission to give seven consecutive performances—that is a week including matinee—and what the fees would be. Your Agent replied giving permission as desired naming fees, and accepting our cheque on account of such fees for these performances without placing any limitation or making any reservation whatever in regard to "Arms and the Man." We thereupon considered the matter arranged and accordingly concluded arrangements to present this play at the Gaiety Theatre for a week, as already stated, and in the event of our failure to carry out this Contract we become liable to the extent of £300. You are, of course, bound by your Agent's contract with us and we have a perfect right, therefore, to give seven consecutive performances as stipulated for. However, with a view to meeting your wishes and in order not to involve you in any difficulty regarding your provincial rights (though we understand that this play has already been performed in Dublin) we got the theatre people to consent to alter the terms of the Contract to four performances of "Arms and the Man" provided we filled up the other three performances with "The Man of Destiny." As we consider this is a reasonable compromise in the circumstances, we hope you will place no further obstacles in the way of this arrangement, otherwise we shall have no alternative but to abide by our Contract with the theatre.

Our reason for playing at the Gaiety is because there is no other place suitable or available, and as a matter of fact, amateur companies usually perform at this theatre. We produced "Hedda Gabler" and "The Doll's House" at the Queen's Theatre, as well as "The Heather Field" (Edward Martyn) and "The Great Galeoto" (Echegaray), playing for a week on each occasion, but this theatre is no longer available as it is now closed and coming down. So you will see that it is no unusual thing for us to play for a week. Indeed we would never have thought of asking for permission to play "Arms and The Man" for a couple of nights, as it would be far too troublesome and expensive for such a short run.

We would further point out, in regard to what you say about first performances of your plays in the provinces, that we believe you gave permission to the Irish National Theatre Society to present "John Bull's Other Island" before a Dublin audience for the first time without any reservation whatever as to the number of performances, besides having already given us permission to play "The Man of Destiny" publicly for the first time here and without any reservation.

With regard to the bona fides of our Club, I may mention that the Players' Club is one of the oldest amateur clubs in Ireland, well known and highly regarded. Mr. George Moore, your contemporary, was at one time our Stage Manager, and is still connected with us. You are not correct in assuming we are inexperienced.

Now, we shall be glad to hear that you will end this unpleasant controversy over a business which has already been definitely concluded, and that you will agree to the compromise which we have been able to effect with the theatre, i.e. to play "Arms and the Man" four nights and "The Man of Destiny" three nights, in order to carry out our engagement.

Awaiting your early reply,

I am,

Yours faithfully,

Anthony Evelyn Ashley.

Hon. Secretary.

George Bernard Shaw, Esq.

COPY

March 6th, 1907.

Dear Sir,

The question at issue—which is of such importance to authors that I shall have to make a test case of it if you seriously claim that you can ask for permission to give an amateur performance and pay amateur fees, and then embark on a commercial theatrical speculation—is whether the week at the Gaiety Theatre is going to be a week of amateur theatricals or a week of ordinary theatrical business. What is the nature of your contract with the Gaiety? Are the terms sharing terms? And if there be a profit where will that profit go to?

Until I am informed on these points I can say nothing more than I have already said. The principle involved is a most important one. It concerns a privilege which is worth, say, twenty guineas in the commercial market and five in the amateur market. To buy the privilege at amateur rates and then exploit it commercially, is a proceeding of which a very strong view indeed would be taken if it were attempted by a regular theatrical manager. I do not suggest that this aspect of the matter occurred to you; but now that I put it plainly before you, you will, I think, see that I am not acting unreasonably. It is quite likely that the net profit on a week of ARMS AND THE MAN may at this moment reach and even considerably exceed £500 if you admit the public by payment at the doors and invite the press. You propose to obtain that profit by paying me a fee fixed on the assumption that there is to be no profit at all and that the enterprise is entirely disinterested as far as money is concerned. Naturally, I refuse to sanction this. If you are an amateur, you must confine yourself to amateur conditions. If you are a man of business, you must pay me business terms.

I hope I do not convey an impression of being unfriendly to your Club; but you will see that it has sprung something on me which was never contemplated when the amateur conditions were fixed.

Yours faithfully,
G. Bernard Shaw.

A. Evelyn Ashley, Esq.
Rathgar, Dublin.

10 Adelphi Terrace, W.C.
1st October 1907.

All my account books, receipt books &c are somewhere in the Great Western luggage trains; and my wife, who usually manipulates them for me, is in Ireland; so I cannot tell you offhand whether the cheque came or not. I have made a note to look into it for you as soon as the books come to hand.

G. B. S.

Miss Elizabeth Marbury,
        20 Green St. Leicester Sq.
        W.C.

_____

10 Adelphi Terrace, W. C.
26th Nov. 1907.

I am told that the Garrick Society of Stockport played to over £ 100 with one of my plays at the Opera House, Buxton, and that they are arranging to give "three consecutive plays" in Liverpool as well as a performance in Oldham. If this is "amateur" business, then all amateur business must be stopped at once. The Liverpool affair is out of the question: it positively must not take place. Please authorize nothing—amateur or otherwise—in future without consulting me. I shall have actions for damages against me presently.

G. B. S.

R. Golding Bright, Esq.,
        Miss Marbury's
            20 Green Street, Leicester Sq.
            W.C.

_____

Ayot St. Lawrence, Welwyn, Herts
Station: Wheathampstead, G.N.R. 2¼ Miles.
Telegrams: Bernard Shaw, Codicote.

27th Nov. 1907.

No: I haven't authorized anybody. My informant is the manager of the Manchester Playgoers Theatre Co., who is touring with "Widowers' Houses."

Did the Stockport Garrick Soc. get leave for the alleged performance in Buxton?

G. B. S.

Reply to Adelphi Terrace: I shall be up tomorrow (Thursday)

R. Golding Bright, Esq.
Miss Marbury's
20 Green Street, Leicester Sq. W.C.

------

10 Adelphi Terrace, W.C.
3rd Jan 1908.

As You Never Can Tell has now been performed by the Vedrenne-Barker Co in Manchester, there is no longer any reason for keeping it locked up in Manchester as far as single performances by amateurs are concerned. Still, be sure that the amateurs are amateurs. I write this because I see it stated in the Mach. Eve. News that the West Didsbury Society (whatever that may be) got choked off Y. N. C. T.—possibly quite rightly; but I thought I'd remind you that a tour had already passed through with Y. N. C. T. & John Bull.

G. B. S.

R. Golding Bright Esq.
c/o Miss Marbury,
20 Green Street, Leicester Sq.
W.C.

Ayot St. Lawrence, Welwyn, Herts.
Station: Wheathampstead, G.N.R. 2¼ Miles.
Telegrams: Bernard Shaw, Codicote.

2nd Feb. 1908.

Unless you hear from me to the contrary before Thursday, you can license the Lincoln people for Brassbound. The delay is to ascertain whether Ellen Terry is going there, in which case I should have to refuse.

The Surrey gentleman is all right. How He Lied and The Man of Destiny count as one full length play. Of course he must play at the place he mentioned, not elsewhere.

G. Bernard Shaw.

Miss Elizabeth Marbury,
20 Green Street, Leicester Sq.
W.C.

Ayot St Lawrence, Welwyn, Herts.
Station: Wheathampstead, G.N.R. 2¼ Miles.
Telegrams: Bernard Shaw, Codicote.

The Woodford people may go ahead. If they wish me to decide what is to be done with the profits (if any) I strongly advise them either to keep them for the promotion of future performances or give them to any public art gallery of the like that may exist at Woodford. Failing that, let them get drunk on it rather than give it to any charity.

G. Bernard Shaw.

Miss Wooldridge   Post Marked
Oc 30 '08.

Miss Elizabeth Marbury
20 Green St, Leicester Sq,
W.C.

Ayot St Lawrence, Welwyn, Herts.
Station: Wheathampstead, G.N.R. 2¼ Miles.
Telegrams: Bernard Shaw, Codicote.

19th June 1909

Major Barbara is not available for amateurs yet.

G. B. S.

Miss Elizabeth Marbury
20 Green St, Leicester Sq.
W.C.

Gt. Southern Hotel, Parknasilla,
Co. Kerry.

In answer to your letter of the 4th, these A.D.C's in Bolton, Liverpool &c, can have the plays for one performance, but not for more. What must be stopped is the snatching of weeks in those towns under pretext of amateurism. In some cases I have found people actually announcing performances without leave under the impression that all they had to do was to send in £5.5.0 afterwards.

G. Bernard Shaw.

Post Marked
Sp. 12 '09.
Co. Kerry.

(Picture)   P O S T   C A R D

Miss Elizabeth Marbury
20 Green St, Leicester Sq. London, W.C.

---

10 Adelphi Terrace, W.C.

Ayot St Lawrence, Welwyn, Herts.
Station: Wheathampstead, G.N.R. 2¼ Miles,
Telegrams: Bernard Shaw, Codicote

2nd November, 1909.

Dear Miss Wooldridge

Whenever people ask for reductions or special privileges of any kind, tell them it is no use—that the fees & conditions of performances are not arranged by the author according to his fancy, but are determined by the whole body of authors acting through the Dramatic Committees of the Society of Authors, and that individual authors are not free to undersell one another by making reductions. The Vaudeville Dramatic Club & the Goldsmiths College (University of London) New Cross must pay the usual fees.

The Green Room Amateur Dramatic Society of Liverpool may play two nights—Thursday and Saturday, NOT the charity night—provided they do not select Arms & The Man or Candida. If they want either play, they can play it once only, as the two are on the road.

The Bolton A.D.C. can have the same reply—Arms & The Man once only.

> Yours faithfully
>
> G. Bernard Shaw.

> 10 Adelphi Terrace
> London, W.C.
> 7th May 1910.

Address Telegrams
to "Socialist London"

Dear Golding Bright

Before I say anything about Major Barbara I must ask Charles Frohman his intentions. He undertook to produce it; but there was no contract. Still, it would be only civil to reopen the subject before I do anything decisive. Also Major Barbara is a play which requires a quite exceptionally strong company, including at least six first-rate people. Laurence Irving had

better write to me direct about it. I doubt very much whether
the play is within his resources.

Yours faithfully,

G. Bernard Shaw.

R. Golding Bright, Esq.,
    Miss Elizabeth Marbury's
        20 Green St., Leicester Sqre., W.C.

---

10 Adelphi Terrace, W.C.

Until the 5th Aug.
Carrigart,
Co. Donegal.

26th July 1910.

Five performances of Press Cuttings is obviously not
amateur business. You had better refer them to me.
I answered about Blackpool before I left London.

G. Bernard Shaw.

I shall be away until October. Letters to Adelphi Terrace
will be forwarded.

Miss Marbury,
20 Green St. Leicester Sq.,
London, W.C.

---

10 Adelphi Terrace, W.C.

Coole Park, Gort, Co. Galway.
16th August 1910.

Bashville, yes.
Barbara, no.

G. B. S.

James W. Milne, 46A Union St. Aberdeen, wants to perform You Never Can Tell—amateur club. Please communicate
with him & authorize on the usual terms.

Miss Marbury,
            20 Green St, Leicester Sq.
            London, W.C.

24th Aug. 1910.
Coole Park, Gort,
Co. Galway.

Manchester—Yes.

Aberdeen—I consent to 2 performances only. Tell them they
must make out a very strong case if they want three, as the
commercial managers rightly regard three performances as a
serious interference with their interests.

I should probably not consent to three in any case.

G. Bernard Shaw.

Miss Marbury,
            20 Green St. Leicester Sq.
            London, W.C.

---

10 Adelphi Terrace, W.C.
8th October 1910.

Address Telegrams
to "Socialist London"

Dear Miss Wooldridge,

In answer to your letter about Sutton and Surbiton, why
do these people want to give three performances? I think you
had better always give a stereotyped reply to people who make
requests of this sort, to the effect that a production for three
nights is outside the usual scope of amateur enterprise, and

that you can only submit the request to me with sufficiently full particulars to convince me that I am really dealing with amateurs and not with professionals, or semi-professionals, or local managers exploiting local amateurs commercially. It is absurd to waste our time in repeating the same correspondence again and again when the answer is always the same. Surbiton is a tolerably important suburb; and if I were to make a contract for, say, Number 3 places with a little professional company, and they found that I have allowed them to be forestalled by these three-night ventures, they would have a very legitimate grievance against me. On the whole, we had better make it a fixed rule that 3 performances are only to be authorized under special circumstances and after very full information.

Yours faithfully,
G. Bernard Shaw.

Miss Elizabeth Marbury,
    20 Green St.,
        Leicester Square, W.C.

    Ayot St Lawrence, Welwyn, Herts.
    Station: Wheathampstead, G.N.R. 2¼ Miles.
    Telegrams: Bernard Shaw, Codicote.

14th Nov. 1911.

Please note that The Doctor's Dilemma is not available for amateurs outside London. Mr. Stanley Houghton says you offered to let him play it for one night in Manchester. Nothing later than John Bull's Other Island has yet been taken round the provinces.

G. Bernard Shaw.

Miss Marbury,
    20 Green Street, Leicester Sq.
        London, W.C.

---

10 Adelphi Terrace, W.C.
2nd January 1913.

Address Telegrams
to "Socialist London"

Dear Golding Bright,

I have to give you notice that on the 25th March next I shall have to transfer the collection of my amateur fees to the Society of Authors.

I am not taking this step because I am dissatisfied with Miss Marbury's services, or on any other ground of dissatisfaction. On the contrary, I think it highly probable that for a year or so at any rate, the arrangement will be to my own disadvantage. But I am not a free agent in this matter. As you probably know, most dramatic authors are, as far as their amateur business is concerned, in the hands of a firm which insists on charging a commission of 20%. The Society of Authors, after several attempts to bring this firm to reason, at last resolved to organize a bureau and undertake the collection of fees for its members. As a member of the Committee of Management I took a leading part in this enterprise, having in the meantime done what I could to persuade other dramatic authors to transfer their business to Miss Marbury. Now that the bureau is organized and in action, it is, you will see, impossible for me to continue having my fees collected by an outside organization.

I have stipulated that I must be allowed to give you three months notice, which I accordingly do, without malice.

Yours faithfully,
G. Bernard Shaw.

Golding Bright, Esq.,
20 Green St.
Leicester Sq. W.C.

18th Feb. 1913.

Ayot St Lawrence, Welwyn, Herts.
Station: Wheathampstead, G.N.R. 2¼ Miles.
Telegrams: Bernard Shaw, Codicote.

Dear Golding Bright

You can let the amateurs loose on Fanny's First Play to their hearts' content. The only difficulty is that it is not yet published; and as I can only lend a single copy, I dont see how performances can be managed until I get my new volume out.

The South African people have been at me about Man & Superman. So have the Dutch people about Fanny. They go to you in despair because I put off answering them for one reason or another. Don't bother about them. In the fullness of time I will attend to them personally.

Yrs ever
G. Bernard Shaw.

---

10 Adelphi Terrace,
London, W.C.
22nd October 1913.

Address Telegrams
to "Socialist Westrand London"

Dear Golding Bright

Pygmalion is not really in the market at present, though I am of course always open to offers. What I mean by this is that though the rights are in my hands and subject to no contract affecting America, yet I have privately made up my mind as to what I am going to do with them. In any case I could not quote general terms. You know roughly that I have often done business at a straight 10% for America and that this may be regarded as a minimum; but a good deal depends on the manager with whom I am dealing. In any case, if the manager does not wish to deal with me directly and approaches me through you, it must be understood that you are acting as his agent and not as mine. As I shall have to do all the work, it is only fair that he should pay all the commission. Anyhow I wont pay any.

I wish you would give up agency and take to honest industry. The older I grow, the more violently I find myself prejudiced against agents of all sorts.

Yours ever,
G. Bernard Shaw.

R. Golding Bright Esq.,
20 Green Street, Leicester Square, W.C.

10 Adelphi Terrace W.C.
19th December 1914.

The Dark Lady of the Sonnets is for the present in Miss Gertrude Kingston's hands who is now in New York arranging for its production with three other plays of mine.

G. Bernard Shaw.

Golding Bright Esq.
20 Green Street,
Leicester Square,
W.C.

Next week Opera House   GRAND   THEATRE
Southport.   BIRMINGHAM.

Jan. 4th, 1916.

My dear Bernard Shaw,
How about your play "Flaherty, V.C."?
I am starting management again at a theatre that I think might interest you. Would you like me to read it; or would you rather see me in hell first?

Yrs etc.
Arthur Bourchier.

Ayot St Lawrence, Welwyn, Herts.
6th Jan. 1916.

My dear Bourchier,

I am sorry to say that the war is an impossible subject for the theatre just now. I have written not only O'F but another little play about it, only to be driven to the conclusion that they would be unbearable. Even Arms & The Man, dating from 1894, jars. It was played on New Year's Day in Scotland before—among others—a colonel home on leave from the front. He said it was quite extraordinary how I knew all about it without any experience, and that Loos was just like the charge at Slivnitza as I described it: "simple suicide: only the pistol did go off" (in the play it didn't); but for that very reason he could hardly stand it. The touch of our art makes the thing live; and nobody could bear the war if it was real to them. Just think of the chance of a piece of bad news on the day of your first night! Excuse my using your letter—war economy!

ever
G. Bernard Shaw.

———————

Ayot St. Lawrence, Welwyn, Herts.
Station: Wheathampstead, G.N.R. 2¼ Miles.
Telegrams: Bernard Shaw, Codicote.

2nd Aug. 1916.

I have received your letter of the 1st Aug, with enclosures as stated.

When my secretary returns from her holiday you shall have the usual acknowledgment.

G. Bernard Shaw.

Miss Elizabeth Marbury,
20 Green St, Leicester Sq.
W.C.

———————

Parknasilla, Kenmore, Co. Kerry.

7/10/17 (until the 13th)

Bless you, there's no need for a MS of O'Flaherty. It has been published in Hearst's Magazine: hence the rush for it. I have plenty of applications.

The agency game is changing. I never employ an agent now: why should I, when the agent does absolutely nothing for me but intercept my fees and send them to me minus 10% for delaying them? If the manager likes to employ an agent, that is his own affair; so long as he pays the agent's commission and it is made clear that the agent is not acting for me, I indulge his imbecility, though I have to advise him, make the agreement, and generally do for him everything that his agent professes to do and doesnt. When I can no longer write plays I will take up agency and become one of the idle rich, instead of envying you with the bitterness of an overworked man.

In the remote past, your American office used to collect my fees. It was not until it became too lazy to do even that, and I had to collect them myself, that I woke up to the situation and discarded agents for ever.

G. B. S.

———————

10 Adelphi Terrace, W.C.
9th October, 1919

Tell William Morris there is no use approaching me.

I have half a dozen solid proposals in figures in my desk made directly to myself; and it is open to any man to add to their number if he feels that way. I am not likely to accept any of them; but the shop is open, and all customers receive respectful attention.

Why not offer to take on the lectures yourself? You could

deliver quite a good set on the theatre, and on London celebrities.

G. Bernard Shaw.

R. Golding Bright, Esq.,
20 Green Street,
Leicester Square,
London, W.C. 2.

The "subsequent plays" mentioned in the first letter meant *Major Barbara* (written 1905, published with *John Bull's Other Island* and *How He Lied*, 1907) and *The Doctor's Dilemma* (written 1906, published with *Getting Married* and *The Shewing-Up of Blanco Posnet*, 1911).... The second paragraph should be compared with the suggested circular sent to Bright a year before, with the letter of February 23, 1906.... The third paragraph, for readers familiar with Shaw's early and persistent knowledge of, interest in, and love for music, is extremely interesting. Leslie Stuart, best known for his music for *Floradora*, was to produce as his next "musical play" *Havana*, with book by George Grossmith Jr. and Graham Herbert, produced at the Gaiety in 1908. It is dubious that Stuart wished Shaw to write the book for this, much more probable that he wished Shaw to write *a* book, which should inspire his melodies. ... Richard D'Oyly Carte needs no introduction, possibly the pun itself is *infra*-Shavian humor, but this news item of information is distinctly interesting, for *Utopia Limited*, produced at the Savoy October 7, 1893, had definitely not been up to Gilbert and Sullivan standards, surpassed actually as failure only by their last collaboration, *The Grand Duke*, opened March 7, 1896. The offer from the Savoy manager here first recorded suggests both his declining faith in his famous team and the strength of Shaw's reputation thus early, based only on his reputation as music critic and probably the quasi- or pseudo-success of *Arms and the Man*, with the resultant crop of reviews in which his humor was compared with Gilbert's, whether justly or not. Robert Courtneidge, director and actor, produced *The Duchess of Dantzig*, a musical version of Sardou's

Madame Sans-Gène, for George Edwardes, the famous "Guv'nor"
of the Gaiety, at the Lyric Theatre, October 17, 1903, with a book
by Henry Hamilton and music by the male star, Ivan Caryll. It was
a great success and Edwardes, according to the producer, thought
it "the best production of a light opera he had ever seen." Here
again is a new and provocative bit of information. Again Shaw's
combined work as critic (review of Irving's and Terry's *Sans-Gène*),
and playwright (*The Man of Destiny*), and the newspaper Irving-
Shaw-Napoleon scandal had obviously brought him to the attention
of a man famous for producing musical plays. . . . For Lowenstein
read Lowenfield. The apparently minor point here involved is
worth emphasis because readers familiar with Shaw's biography
will know the name of Dr. F. E. Loewenstein, who from 1936
worked on the definitive Shaw bibliography and from 1944 to
Shaw's death in 1950 worked at Shaw's Corner daily. The producer
referred to by Shaw in 1907 was Henry Lowenfield, a manager who
in 1901 opened the Apollo, next door to Edwardes' Lyric, and there
starred such famous figures as Edna May, Evie Greene, G. P.
Huntley, and Hayden Coffin. . . . The last sentence of the letter is
not entirely a joke. Shaw, who in his nineties could play the scores
and sing the arias from his favorite operas, probably did have both
the desire and the capacity to compose.

- - - - - - - - - -

The items from Shaw's note to Ada Wooldridge of February
27th through the copy of his letter to Anthony Evelyn Ashley,
secretary of the Irish Players' Club, of March 6th, 1907, give considerable insight into the tea-pot tempests both of amateur producing groups and of playwrights interested enough in all productions to prevent their relying wholly upon their agents' dealings.
Probably the flurry over the particular matter was the greater
since the chief participants were all belligerently Irish. (I assume
the very English-sounding secretary *was* Irish. Why not? With my
name, I am.) . . . With reference to Ashley's letter to Shaw, a few
comments might be in order. The two novelists and good friends,
Edward Martyn, mentioned as playwright, and George Moore, mentioned as stage manager for the Players' Club, were associated as
early as 1891 with Yeats in the Irish Literary Society and with
subsequent groups interested in the founding of a national theatre

in Ireland. The Irish Literary Theatre, founded in January, 1899, sponsored by Yeats and Martyn, presented Yeats' *The Countess Cathleen* and Martyn's *The Heather Field* in May of that year. So far as permission of the Irish National Theatre Society to produce *John Bull's Other Island* is concerned, Ashley's argument is weak. Shaw actually wrote the play at the request of Yeats for the Literary Theatre, but it was turned down in the spring of 1905 on the ground that its production would be too expensive, and so it was produced instead at the Court in London and by Arnold Daly in New York.

. . . .

The unrewarding business note of October 1, 1907, to Miss Marbury, has a certain interest for the Shavian scholar since on her Irish visit Charlotte Shaw first saw Forbes Robertson play her husband's Caesar, her firm "favorite among all my husband's character studies," and found his performance "one of the finest things I ever have seen upon the stage." On November 1st, Shaw wrote to the actor that she returned to London "in a state of insanity about you," and gave his own opinion that it was "flatly impossible that any human actor could be so out of the way splendid as she reports you to have been."

. . . .

The famous address, "Ayot St. Lawrence, Welwyn, Herts," appears for the first time on the brief note to Bright of November 27, 1907. In 1906 the Shaws had moved their country residence to the New Rectory there, which they bought and which became famous as Shaw's Corner.

. . . .

With reference to the note of May 7, 1910, concerning *Major Barbara*, I find that the play was not performed in America until December 9, 1915, when William A. Brady produced it at his Playhouse for his wife Grace George. Five of the "at least six first-rate" parts are clearly identifiable as Lady Britomart, Barbara, Ousins, Undershaft, and Bill Walker. Who was Shaw's own sixth? The reader, producer, or player has a choice of at least six others for this place: Stephen, Rummy Mitchens, Snobby Price, Jenny Hill, Peter Shirley, or Mrs. Baines. . . . Laurence Irving, second son of

Sir Henry, never produced the play. He had played Captain Brassbound for the Stage Society's two performances in 1900; otherwise,
to my knowledge, he essayed no Shavian roles.

- - - - - - - - - -

Press Cuttings, mentioned in the note to Miss Marbury, July 26,
1910, was a pro-suffragette one-act piece written by Shaw in 1909.
He described it as "A Topical Sketch Compiled from the Editorial
and Correspondence Columns of the Daily Papers during the
Woman's War in 1909." The play was refused a license, so the
suffragettes founded a society called The Civic and Dramatic Guild
and presented it at a "Private Reception" at the Court for two performances in July. In September Miss A. E. F. Horniman's company gave seven performances at the Gaiety Theatre in Manchester.
In June, 1910 a benefit matinée performance was given at the
Kingsway Theatre, London, by the Actresses' Franchise League.
. . . The refusal of license was explained on the ground that the
satiric portraits of General Mitchener and Prime Minister Balsquith
too obviously suggested lampoons on Kitchener-and-Milner and
Asquith-and-Balfour; so Shaw changed the names, with blatant
sarcasm, to the minstrel end-men's names of Bones and Johnson,
and, amazingly, the Censor passed the play.

- - - - - - - - - -

The note of November 14, 1911, to Miss Marbury, concerning
Stanley Houghton's desire to produce *The Doctor's Dilemma* with
amateurs at Manchester, might easily confuse readers familiar with
Miss Horniman's Gaiety company, definitely not an amateur group.
But at the date of this note, Houghton was still working on his
most famous play, *Hindle Wakes,* and one assumes his request was
made on behalf of the Manchester Athenaeum Dramatic Society,
for which he frequently acted as producer and of which he was
for a time secretary. He was himself a devoted amateur actor, playing, according to Harold Brighouse, over seventy parts from 1901
to 1912, including Sergius Saranoff in *Arms and the Man* and
William the Waiter in *You Never Can Tell.*

- - - - - - - - - -

The letter to Bright of January 2, 1913, while not of exciting content, is important because it explains why the correspondence was so soon to dwindle, to skip several years, and suddenly, apparently, to stop, over thirteen years before the death of Bright, and almost twenty-three before that of Shaw. . . . Always interested in any organization or union of specialized workers, Shaw eagerly joined such groups as the Society of Authors or the Dramatists' Club. Blanche Patch, his long-time secretary, in her *Thirty Years with G.B.S.*, tells (pp. 136-139) of how he had 1,500 words of advice to young playwrights set up and printed on galley proofs for answering any inquiries (an even greater, if less personal, sign of his generosity and tolerance than his *Advice to a Young Critic*); in this he advised as a first step joining the Society of Authors. For this group he served not only on the Committee of Management but also on the Dramatic Sub-Committee. Notice how carefully he made clear that his decision "to transfer the collection of . . . amateur fees," from Miss Marbury's office was made not for personal reasons, but for the general good of his fellow-craftsmen. March 25, 1913, was given as the date for his severing relations with the Marbury agency. It will be seen that all communications after that date have to do with American rights or with special and unusual questions.

- - - - - - - - - -

Fanny's First Play, mentioned in the note of February 18, 1913, had been written in 1911, and presented, under Shaw's direction, by Lillah McCarthy at the Little Theatre, April 19th of that year. Transferred to the Kingsway on the following New Year's Day, it ran in all for 622 performances, still the record for a Shaw play. Until it was published in 1914 with *Misalliance* and *The Dark Lady of the Sonnets*, Shaw kept up the pretense of anonymity which he adopted when it was first produced, when it was announced as by Xxxxxxx Xxxx. The pretense, however, from the first, deceived nobody.

- - - - - - - - - -

The note of October 22, 1913, is the first written to Bright after Shaw had formally severed relations. Typically he urges his former protégé to "give up agency and take to honest industry." But Golding Bright found it the work he wanted and was suited for, and

he practised it up to his death. *Pygmalion,* actually written for
Mrs. Pat Campbell during 1912 and 1913, was first produced in
Vienna, starring Lilli Marberg and Max Paulsen, a week before
this note was written. Like so many of its predecessors, this play,
despite its later popularity, had to wait some months for production. It was started as a result of George Alexander's request for a
play one night during the run of *Bella Donna,* starring Mrs. Pat
and himself. When Alexander saw the script he immediately per-
ceived its worth, and offered to produce it with any actress of
Shaw's choice *except* the one for whom he had created Eliza Doo-
little. Next Mrs. Pat affected to be insulted by the part. Then she
refused to consider Robert Loraine, whom Shaw wanted for Hig-
gins. Finally it was produced for a run of 118 performances by
Beerbohm Tree at His Majesty's, beginning April 11, 1914. Shaw
himself most amusingly described the hectic rehearsal period and
its aftermath in an essay contributed to Max Beerbohm's collection
of memoirs of his brother. I do not know what American manager
was inquiring about the play before its London production. Actually Liebler and Co. (or George C. Tyler) managed the American
première, with Mrs. Pat and Philip Merivale, who had played
Colonel Pickering in the London production.

- - - - - - - - - - -

The brief note of December 19, 1914, obviously relates to another American inquiry, concerning *The Dark Lady of the Sonnets,*
a one-act written in 1910 at the suggestion of Dame Edith Lyttelton
and presented at two charity matinées at the Haymarket, November
24th and 25th, by the Committee of the Shakespeare Memorial
National Theatre. . . . Gertrude Kingston, for whom Shaw wrote
Great Catherine in 1913 (produced at the Vaudeville, November
18th) was always a great favorite with the playwright. She had
also played Aurora Bompas at the Court in *How He Lied to Her
Husband* in February, 1905, and in America she produced the short
piece satirizing the Kaiser, *The Inca of Perusalem,* at the Neighborhood Playhouse, November 14, 1916, and the short farce *Overruled* (written in 1912) at the Toy Theatre, Boston, February 15,
1915, and at the Maxine Elliott in New York, February 2, 1917.
She repeated *Great Catherine* in America at the Boston Toy Theatre following *Overruled* and played it together with *The Inca* at

the Neighborhood. I have not been able to find record of her American appearance in *The Dark Lady*. The delay in production from the time she was in New York arranging matters from the date of the note was obviously a result of World War I conditions.

. . . .

The entries of January 4 and 6, 1916, from and to Arthur Bourchier, concern *O'Flaherty, V.C.*, written in 1915 as a "recruiting pamphlet" to be performed by the Abbey Theatre. It is a delightful piece of spoofing, but one is not surprised that it was not judged "suitable" for its purpose, since beneath its fun there runs an expected Shavian vein of attack upon war and militarism. Shaw's good friend and interpreter, Robert Loraine, produced it and the other "little play" about the war on February 17, 1917, at Treizennes, Belgium, where he was in command of the 40th R. F. C. Squadron. The officers presented *O'Flaherty*, with Loraine in the title role; the men, *The Inca of Perusalem*. Shaw, on an official visit to the Western Front, visited a dress rehearsal. The play was presented by the Deborah Bierne Irish Players at the 39th Street Theatre, New York, for sixteen performances beginning June 21, 1920, and was given twice by the Stage Society in December of that year at the Lyric Theatre, Hammersmith, London.

. . . .

In connection with the note of October 9, 1919, I have not been able to trace when the William Morris referred to went into business as agent for actors and lecturers, but the William Morris Agency is still in business in 1955, handling the affairs, for instance, of one of 1955's most prosperous entertainers, Frank Sinatra.

107. The True History of *The Chocolate Soldier*

10 Adelphi Terrace,
London, W.C. 2.
17th October 1925.

Dear Golding Bright

Nobody but myself has any rights whatever in Arms and the Man.

The history of The Chocolate Soldier, as far as I am concerned in it, is this. I saw a press paragraph to the effect that Oscar Strauss was making a musical version of Arms and the Man. I wrote to him warning him not to infringe my rights. He did not reply; but soon afterwards I received an appeal ad misericordium from Herr Jacobson not to ruin him by forbidding the performance of The Chocolate Soldier, as he had written the libretto, of which he sent me a copy. I read it, and found that he had used certain scraps of my dialogue, the effect of which in the context of his stuff was so bad that I improved the piece considerably by cutting them all out. I then told him I would have nothing whatever to do with The Chocolate Soldier; but if none of my dialogue was used I did not think I could appeal to the courts successfully to stop the performance, because (a) parodies and travesties of standard serious works are privileged by custom, (b) I had clearly no rights in the Servo-Bulgarian war as a dramatic subject, and (c) the incident of a fugitive soldier taking refuge in a lady's bedroom was too common to be patented by me or anyone else. There were no other features in The Chocolate Soldier apart from the title which could be found in Arms and the Man. Jacobson's

characters were all cads, cowards, vieux marcheurs, and prostitutes with names invented by himself. His libretto was not a
play, but a putrid opéra bouffe in the worst taste of 1860. Under
these circumstances I did not propose to take any steps provided my name was not connected with the thing in any way.

Even with this Herr Jacobson was not satisfied. He pleaded
that he would be accused of plagiarism if he were not allowed
to say that he had borrowed an incident from Arms and the
Man; and I said that he might say what he liked provided he
conveyed no suggestion that I was in any way responsible for
his libretto, or that Oscar Strauss's score was a setting of Arms
and the Man.

I never departed from this attitude. It was evident that they
all believed that I could have stopped The Chocolate Soldier,
because they all offered to pay me a royalty. Mr. Whitney, who
produced the play in America, was very anxious about me, as it
seemed unaccountable that I should refuse money when there
was so much of it going. But it was just because there was so
much money in it that I did not stop it. It gave a lot of employ-
ment to the artists and others, and plenty of enjoyment to the
public. Then there was Strauss to be considered. He was not to
blame, as he evidently knew nothing about the copyright question. So I let them alone; and they all flourished exceedingly.

I believe I told Miss Marbury to come down on them if they
used any of my dialogue in the American version; but as she
was not collecting any fees for me she had no interest in the
matter, and took no action. I afterwards found that some of
my dialogue had been used.

Now that the film question has arisen over the success of the
Theatre Guild production of Arms and the Man I shall probably deal with it just as I did with The Chocolate Soldier. If
they make a film of The Chocolate Soldier by Strauss, Jacobson
& Co, I may not meddle with them. But if they bring my name
into it, or connect it with Arms and the Man in any way, then
I shall come down on them at once.

I cannot, however, answer for the attitude of the Theatre Guild. It may object to the release of a film called The Chocolate Soldier as an infringement of their interest in the play; and they might possibly get an injunction.

In any case Mr. Rumsey will not find it worth his while to interfere, as I will not be bought off by a royalty or anything of that sort, and there will therefore be nothing for him to collect. I shall instruct my American lawyer to warn Mr. Goldwin, and also put the Theatre Guild on its guard.

By the way, I shall have to take the amateur business out of the hands of Miss Marbury (that is, I suppose, out of the hands of the American Play Company) if I do not receive my fees regularly as I used to. My American Income Tax returns were upset last time by a quite inexcusable delay. Perhaps they will wake up if you jog them.

Faithfully
G. Bernard Shaw.

R. Golding Bright Esq.,
Miss Elizabeth Marbury,
20 Green Street,
Leicester Square,
W.C.2.

Much has been written throughout the years by innumerable Shavian critics and biographers concerning the relationship of the popular operetta by Oscar Strauss to *Arms and the Man;* but no comment has been so full or so detailed as this one, straight from the lion's mouth. Strauss's operetta was produced in Berlin in 1909 and at the Lyric, London, in 1910, when the program bore the note: "With apologies to Mr. Bernard Shaw for an unauthorized parody on one of his comedies." . . . The fullest chronological history of the writing and productions of *Der Tapfere Soldat* (literally *The Gallant Soldier*) will be found in Archibald Henderson's *Playboy and Prophet,* in a footnote on pp. 475-476, too long even to resume here. . . . The Theatre Guild production referred to had opened about a month before, at the Guild Theatre, September 14, 1925. It had starred Lynn Fontanne and Alfred Lunt, with a strong supporting cast including Ernest Cossart, Henry Travers, and Pedro de Cordoba. . . . The matter of the filming of *The Chocolate Soldier* was not to be so easily dismissed as Shaw imagined when sending Bright this letter. In 1927, Shaw was involved in a fairly silly lawsuit, described in detail by Blanche Patch, *Thirty Years with G.B.S.*, pp. 204-206, brought by an American (unnamed by Miss Patch) who claimed that he had bought film rights to the operetta but was prevented by Shaw from filming. Shaw was awarded £800 damages which he never bothered to collect. . . . Herein is the first reference in this correspondence to the American Play Company, which had been formed in 1914 when Miss Marbury, made first vice-president, pooled her interests with those of several other New York play and actors' agents.

108. Reprise to *Arms and The Man*

4, Whitehall Court,
London, S.W.1.
19th January 1928.

Telegrams:
Socialist, Parl-London.

My dear G.B.

In reply to yours of the 30th December asking on behalf of your New York office whether I am prepared to negotiate for the world film rights of Arms and the Man, I am prepared to negotiate with anybody about anything in the course of my business provided the anybody is a principal or the agent of the principal, and is not proposing to negotiate as my agent.

As you may imagine I do not need introductions to the film firms: they come to me when they mean business. You had better tell your New York people that there is nothing for them in it.

I have no objection on principle to be filmed; but I have to consider the effect on my ordinary theatrical business; and my general policy is to wait until I have had a revival which shelves the play for five years or so before putting it on the filmable list. Also this Movietone development is complicating the question a good deal.

Ever
G. Bernard Shaw.

R. Golding Bright, Esq.
American Play Company
20 Green Street
Leicester Square
W.C.2.

It pleases me as editor of this collection of Shaviana that the last recorded letter to Bright should bear the cordial beginning "My dear G.B." for the first time, that it should be signed "Ever" (why not G.B.S.?), that these last two entries should so happily by coincidence return to a discussion of the play whose first production had brought the young critic so publicly and so privately to Shaw's attention, that this last letter should be concerned with the filming, not of *The Chocolate Soldier,* but of *Arms and the Man* itself, that —by another coincidence—that play should have been the first full-length Shaw play to be filmed (the first was the one-acter, *How He Lied to Her Husband,* in 1930) in 1932, directed by Cecil Lewis, and supervised by Shaw, and that about six months from the date of this last letter, Shaw was one of the first "greats" to appear and talk on Movietone, not for any special occasion but simply because he was G.B.S.